MANAGING YOUR ARTHRITIS

MANAGING YOUR ARTHRITIS

MARY ANNE DUNKIN

Chief Medical Editor
John H. Klippel, MD

CLASS PUBLISHING • LONDON

The authors and publishers welcome feedback from the users of this book. Please contact the publishers.
Class Publishing Ltd, Barb House, Barb Mews, London W6 7PA
Telephone: 020 7371 2119 Fax: 020 7371 2878 [International +4420]
Email: post@class.co.uk

Notice: The information presented in this book is accurate and current to the best of the author's and publisher's knowledge. The author and publisher, however, make no guarantee as to, and assume no responsibility for, the correctness, sufficiency or completeness of such information or recommendation. The reader is advised to consult a doctor regarding all aspects of individual health care.

A CIP catalogue record for this book is available from the British Library.

ISBN 978 1 85959 121 5

Original editorial director: Susan Bernstein
Original art director: Susan Siracusa
Original production artist: Darryl Moland
Original art: Kathryn Born

UK edition
Edited by Gillian Clarke
Indexed by Michèle Clarke

Printed and bound in Slovenia by Delo Tiskarna
by arrangement with Korotan, Ljubljana

ABOUT THE AUTHOR

Mary Anne Dunkin is an experienced journalist specializing in arthritis and related diseases, and other medical topics. She served as Senior Editor for *Arthritis Today* magazine for six years, and currently works as a contributing editor to the magazine. Ms. Dunkin and her family live in suburban Atlanta. This is her first book.

ACKNOWLEDGMENTS

The Arthritis Foundation's Guide to Managing Your Arthritis is written for people who have arthritis or other related diseases, as well as for their friends, family and loved ones. Bringing this book to completion was a team effort, including the significant contributions of dedicated physicians, health-care professionals, Arthritis Foundation volunteers, writers, editors, designers and Arthritis Foundation staff.

Special acknowledgments should go to Mary Anne Dunkin, the author of the book. The chief medical editor of the book was John H. Klippel, MD, the Medical Director of the Arthritis Foundation. The book was reviewed by James R. O'Dell, MD, of the Department of Internal Medicine at the University of Nebraska Medical Center in Omaha; Lee S. Simon, MD, of the Department of Medicine at Beth Israel Deaconness Medical Center in Boston; and E. William St. Clair, MD, of the Department of Medicine at Duke University Medical Center in Durham, NC. The author would also like to thank Doyt Conn, MD, Professor of Medicine, Director of Allergy, Immunology and Rheumatology at Emory University School of Medicine in Atlanta, for his guidance during the writing of this book.

> This book is the updated and extended UK version of *The Arthritis Foundation's Guide to Managing Your Arthritis*, and has been adapted for the United Kingdom with the co-operation of Arthritis Care.

Contents

FOREWORD
TO THE US EDITION

Arthritis is one of the most common diseases affecting Americans today – nearly 66 million people in this country live with some form of arthritis. Arthritis strikes people of all ages, including children, and the number of people with arthritis is expected to increase by millions in the future. Arthritis is not just one disease, but more than 100 different disorders that affect joints, muscles, tendons, and in many instances internal organs of the body. All forms of arthritis impact people's lives in profound ways ranging from the limited activities caused by pain or inability to fully use a joint affected by arthritis, to severe and even life-threatening complications associated with many forms of arthritis.

There are four key steps for successful treatment of all forms of arthritis. First, learn as much as you can about arthritis and treatment options available to you. Second, make a decision to do something about the arthritis. Third, see a doctor to learn what type of arthritis you have. Finally, work with your doctor to develop a plan of treatment.

Arthritis treatment is very much dependent on the type of arthritis being treated. For example, osteoarthritis (the most common form of arthritis) is treated very differently from rheumatoid arthritis, lupus or fibromyalgia. Moreover, most forms of arthritis are chronic. Treatment needs and goals typically change over time, and require a close working relationship between the person with arthritis, their doctor, and other members of a health-care team for success of the treatment.

There are now a number of very effective approaches available for the person with arthritis. Regular exercise, weight control and avoiding injury to joints are important for essentially all forms of arthritis, particularly osteoarthritis. Medications, including both over-the-counter and prescription drugs, play an important role in pain management. Over the past decade, there have been major advances in new medicines available for arthritis treatment. In addition, there has been a tremendous interest and increase in the use of alternative or complementary medicines for arthritis. Finally, surgery to replace joints irreversibly damaged by arthritis has become an almost routine procedure when a person's arthritis has made them practically immobile.

This book, *The Arthritis Foundation's Guide to Managing Your Arthritis*, gives you the tools you will need to understand your arthritis treatment and to take control to more effectively manage your arthritis. In these pages, you will learn about the most common forms of arthritis, their many symptoms, how your doctor will diagnose your disease and how you will work with your health-care professional to begin a course of treatment. You will learn about the many drugs, surgical therapies and alternative approaches to treating arthritis. Most importantly, you will learn how your actions will impact your health – from exercise to diet to stress and pain management. This book will help you take control of arthritis – instead of allowing arthritis to take control of your life.

The Arthritis Foundation believes that the actions taken by people with arthritis play a large and important role in determining their outcome. Education, self-management and taking personal responsibility are tools of empowerment and keys to achieving control of arthritis. *The Arthritis Foundation's Guide to Managing Your Arthritis* is a practical and clear guide that will help you achieve a healthier, more fulfilling life with arthritis.

John H. Klippel, MD
Medical Director
Arthritis Foundation
Atlanta, GA

FOREWORD
TO THE UK EDITION

Arthritis affects every family in the UK. With one in five people living with some form of the condition, it is not only the most common chronic disease but also the biggest cause of physical disability. Yet all too often it is neglected or played down. Harmful myths still prevail: that it is a disease of old age, to be 'put up with', that there is nothing much that can be done. Such notions are nonsense and this book seeks to set the record straight.

Arthritis is a family of over 200 conditions that can affect our bones and joints, often involving severe pain and immobility when left untreated. One myth-busting fact is that over 12,000 children in the UK have arthritis: I was just three years old when I contracted juvenile arthritis. The most common form, osteoarthritis, can also strike early, although it does, of course, affect older people more frequently. With people living longer, society ignores the challenge of arthritis at its peril: the 1:5 incidence is set to rise markedly.

The good news is that there is now a lot that people with arthritis can do to manage their condition. Advice about how diet, gentle exercise and weight control can improve well-being is more widely available than ever. Whilst there is still no cure for arthritis, treatments have also improved enormously (especially for inflammatory forms such as rheumatoid arthritis).

So governments and health services are finally waking up to the fact that arthritis is manageable. Health professionals, be they GPs, rheumatologists, physiotherapists or whoever, are also recognising that supporting people to manage their arthritis themselves is the only sensible way forward. We are 'patients' for a fraction of our lives but the arthritis never deserts us.

In the meantime we want just what everybody else does: to have an education, to have fun, to work, to develop relationships – to live our own lives.

At Arthritis Care, we believe that this means getting the right information to help you make the choices that are right for you. I hope this book goes at least some way to helping you do that.

Neil Betteridge
Chief Executive
Arthritis Care

Introduction

You probably are reading this book because you or someone you love has arthritis. You're not alone. Arthritis is one of the most common medical conditions affecting us today, and as the population ages, the numbers of people affected by arthritis are only going to increase. At the time of this book's publication, an estimated 9 million people in the UK have some form of arthritis or a related disease.

Although the prevalence of certain forms of arthritis increases with age, arthritis is not just a disease of older people. In fact, arthritis is not a disease at all, but a term used to refer to more than 200 related conditions that can cause pain, stiffness, swelling, inflammation and damage to joints and surrounding tissues. Arthritis in its various forms can affect anyone of any age, causing altered growth, time away from school and work, and difficulty performing basic daily tasks.

But the prognosis is not all bleak – far from it! Proper treatment can relieve pain and other symptoms and, in some cases, slow or halt the disease process. Never before have doctors had so many options to offer people with arthritis, and advances in treatment are occurring at an unprecedented pace.

In the past, many people with arthritis believed that their role in treatment was passive. They believed that there was little they could do except take the medications their doctor prescribed, have surgery if necessary and learn to live with the pain, stiffness, limited mobility and other symptoms associated with their disease. This passive role left them feeling out of control, and often allowed arthritis to take over their lives.

Now, when people are first diagnosed with arthritis, their doctors tell them that the most important thing a person with a chronic illness must do is take control. People with arthritis must take an active role in their treatment, a practice known as *self-management*. Self-managers work with their rheumatologists and other health-care professionals in a partnership of care, asking questions, keeping track of pain and other symptoms, engaging in healthy lifestyle practices and exploring various options for treatment. Self-management includes taking an active role while you are in the doctor's office as well as in daily life.

In addition to faithfully taking the medications you have been prescribed – and alerting your doctor to medication-related problems – you can take many measures to ease your symptoms and live well with arthritis. These methods cover a wide range, from exercise and proper diet to mind–body techniques that reduce pain and stress. In this book, you'll learn the basics for many of these methods and techniques. You will learn important information about the causes and symptoms of arthritis, the most common arthritis drugs and surgical therapies, and self-management strategies that will help you control pain and other problems. Although you may need the help of a professional to get you started, you can take control of your treatment.

Whether you are new to arthritis or have lived with it for years, this book should have something to help you. You'll find information for every step of your journey with arthritis, from getting a diagnosis to assembling a health-care team to evaluating arthritis information on the Internet to recuperating from surgery, if that action is necessary. Let this book challenge you to learn more about your condition, open the lines of communication with your doctor, work in partnership with your health-care team and take steps to find out what works for you.

The concept of being responsible for managing your arthritis may seem overwhelming at first, especially if you grew up in an era when patients unquestioningly followed doctors' orders. With some practical advice, encouragement and a little time, the concept can be liberating. You can do something about your arthritis, and this book is a great way to get started.

PART ONE

UNDERSTANDING ARTHRITIS

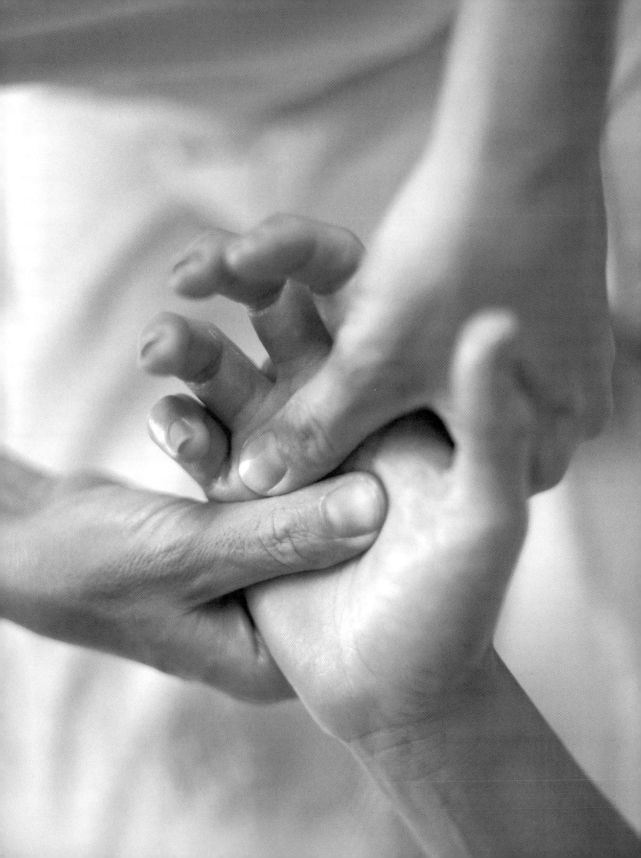

What Is Arthritis?

1

CHAPTER 1: WHAT IS ARTHRITIS?

Mention the word arthritis and many people think of the aches and pains that occur naturally with age. If you have arthritis yourself, you probably know all too well that it's much more than aches and pains, there's nothing natural about it, and you don't have to be old to have it. Furthermore, arthritis technically is not an 'it' but a whole collection of related diseases.

While often referred to as if it were a single disease, arthritis is actually an umbrella term used for a group of more than 200 medical conditions that collectively affect nearly 9 million people of all ages in the UK. While the most common form of arthritis – osteoarthritis (OA) – is most prevalent in people over age 60, arthritis in its various forms can start as early as infancy. Some forms affect people in their young-adult years as they are beginning careers and families and still others start during the peak career and child-rearing years.

The common thread among these 200-plus conditions is that they all affect the musculo-skeletal system and specifically the *joints* – where two or more bones meet (see diagrams below). Arthritis-related joint problems include pain, stiffness, inflammation and damage to joint cartilage (the tough, smooth tissue that covers the ends of the bones, enabling them to glide against one another) and surrounding structures. Such damage can lead to joint weakness, instability and visible deformities that, depending on the location of joint involvement, can interfere with the most basic daily tasks such as walking, climbing

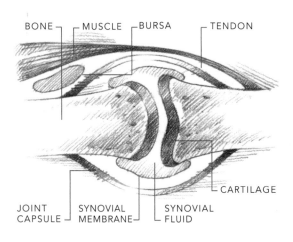

A NORMAL JOINT

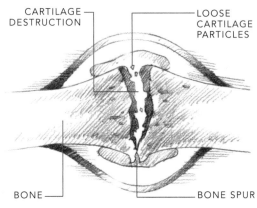

A JOINT WITH OSTEOARTHRITIS

WHAT IS A JOINT?

The joints, which link our 206 bones, are among the body's most ingenious structures and make almost any type of movement possible.

Some joints, such as the elbows and knees, are called hinge joints. They move back and forth like an opening and closing door. Ball-and-socket joints, such as the hip or shoulder, enable bones to twist and turn in many directions while staying firmly connected to each other. Other joints, such as those of the pelvis, move little, and some, such as the joints of the skull, where rigidity is desirable, don't move at all.

Despite their many marvels, joints have their limits. While they thrive with use, excessive use can be harmful. They are also subject to damage – through either trauma or any of the 200-plus forms of arthritis. In understanding arthritis, it helps to have a basic knowledge of what a joint is and the structures that make up a joint.

Basically, a joint is where two or more bones meet. Our bodies have close to 150 of those junctures. Covering the ends of those bones is a smooth, rubbery tissue called *cartilage* that acts as a shock absorber and allows the joint to move smoothly. Some joints are cushioned by small, fluid-filled sacs, called *bursae*. The entire joint is enclosed in capsule composed of tough connective tissue and lined with a thin membrane called the *synovium*. The synovium secretes a viscous, or slippery, liquid called synovial fluid. That fluid lubricates the joints, making movement easier.

Surrounding and supporting your joints are soft tissues, including *muscles*, which are made up of stretchable fibres that help move parts of the body; *tendons*, which are fibres at the ends of muscles that connect them to the bones; and *ligaments*, which are supporting tissues that attach to bones and help keep them together at a joint.

Depending on the particular form of arthritis you have, almost any of these structures – from the cartilage and synovium inside the joint to the ligaments and tendons that support the joint – can be affected.

stairs, using a computer keyboard, cutting your food or brushing your teeth.

For many people with arthritis, however, joint involvement is not the extent of the problem. Many forms of arthritis are classified as *systemic*, meaning they can affect the whole body. In these diseases, arthritis can cause damage to virtually any bodily organ or system, including the heart, lungs, kidneys, blood vessels and skin. Arthritis-related conditions primarily affect the muscles and bones.

Together, arthritis and related conditions are a major cause of disability in the UK, costing the economy a great deal in medical care and indirect expenses such as lost wages and production – and costing millions of individuals their health, their physical abilities and, in many cases, their independence. And unless something changes, the picture is going to get worse. As the population ages, the number of people with arthritis is growing.

There is good news for people with arthritis. Things are changing. While the number of people with arthritis is increasing, in general, these people are faring better than at any time in history. While there is currently no cure for arthritis, most forms can be managed successfully with available medication and non-medication treatments. In the meantime, research is leading to a better understanding of arthritis-related diseases, better ways to diagnose them and more, better and safer treatments for them.

Research is also helping to identify genes involved in different forms of arthritis. For example, a decade ago, researchers found a gene mutation that was responsible for a defect in type II collagen, a major component of joint cartilage. The gene mutation, they found, ran in families and caused defective cartilage that is prone to breakdown. As a result, people with the mutation developed premature osteoarthritis – often by their 20s.

While the link between genes and other forms of arthritis is less clear, most arthritis-related diseases – if not all – are believed to have a genetic component. In many of them, genetic markers have been identified. But that doesn't mean that you will develop a certain form of arthritis just because a parent, sibling, aunt or uncle has it. It is likely that a number of genes, along with other factors such as a virus, bacterium or something else in the environment, cause the development of arthritis in certain people.

By identifying and better understanding the involved genes, doctors hope not only to create better treatments for arthritis but also to be able to target treatment at people with the greatest risk of severe disease. The hope is that early, aggressive treatment in combination with lifestyle modifications (such as losing excess pounds or limiting activities that would put undue stress on arthritis-susceptible joints) may help minimize or even prevent some types of arthritis-related joint damage.

What Kind of
Arthritis Do I Have?

2

CHAPTER 2: WHAT KIND OF ARTHRITIS DO I HAVE?

If you have experienced joint pain, stiffness, swelling or inflammation, you may have arthritis. You probably picked up this book because you suspect that you or someone you love has arthritis. But what type of arthritis could it be?

As discussed in Chapter 1, arthritis is not a single disease, although the term is often used as if it is. Instead, arthritis refers to more than 200 different forms of the disease and related conditions. The similarity among the different forms is that they affect the joints, generally causing pain. Arthritis and related conditions may cause pain and damage to the connective tissue of the muscles, ligaments, tendons, bones, skin and internal organs.

Discussing all of the different forms of arthritis and related conditions is beyond the scope of this book, and most forms of the disease are quite rare. In this chapter, you'll learn about some of the most common forms and related conditions. You may think you recognize your condition from these descriptions, and you may be right. But arthritis cannot be diagnosed by reading a book. If you don't have a diagnosis from a doctor, it's important that you see one. Different forms of arthritis usually are treated differently; you may need to see a *rheumatologist* (a doctor who specializes in arthritis) to get the specialized care you need. Ultimately, prompt and proper treat-

ment offers the best chance to prevent damage and complications of the disease.

OSTEOARTHRITIS

Osteoarthritis (OA), the most common form of arthritis, affects around eight out of ten people over the age of 50 although it can also affect younger people. In its early stages, osteoarthritis can be difficult to detect – some people are not aware that they have it, or only become aware of it when symptoms develop. Like many other forms of arthritis, it is more common in women than in men.

If you have osteoarthritis, you probably experience morning stiffness and mild to

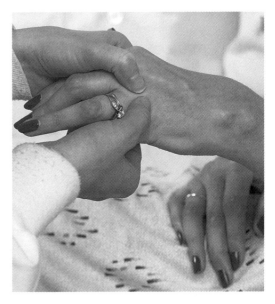

moderate pain that may come on slowly throughout the day or may come and go periodically. On the other hand, you may have pain and stiffness that steadily worsen, making it difficult to go about your daily life.

The pain of OA is usually in or around the affected joints, which most commonly are joints of the knees, hips, fingers, neck and lower back. Knuckles, wrists, elbows, shoulders and ankles are affected very rarely. If osteoarthritic joint changes cause pressure on the nerves and muscles surrounding the joint, the pain may be felt elsewhere, a problem known as referred pain. For example, osteoarthritis in the neck may be felt as pain in the shoulder.

Deformities due to overgrowth of bone at the margins of the joint are common in osteoarthritis, particularly in the fingers. Knobby bone growths in the finger joints nearest the nails are called *Heberden's nodes*, and growths in the middle of the fingers are called *Bouchard's nodes*, named for the doctors

who first described them (see diagram below.) Such growths tend to run in families and are more common in women than in men. The nodes may appear on only one finger or on several fingers. They may cause chronic or intermittent pain and interfere with the ability to enjoy such leisure activities as needlework, playing the piano or golfing.

Until recently, osteoarthritis was considered a normal part of the ageing process; it was believed that joint cartilage naturally deteriorated after years of use. Increasingly, however, doctors believe that OA is not an inevitable part of ageing. They now realize that OA may result from a number of factors, including:

• **Genetic defects in cartilage.** At least one genetic abnormality, a mutation of a gene that codes for Type II collagen, a major component of joint cartilage, has been associated with OA in certain people with premature development of the disease.

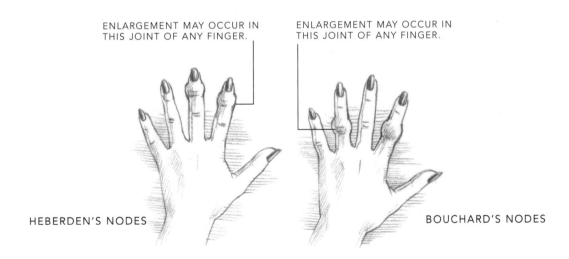

ENLARGEMENT MAY OCCUR IN THIS JOINT OF ANY FINGER.

ENLARGEMENT MAY OCCUR IN THIS JOINT OF ANY FINGER.

HEBERDEN'S NODES

BOUCHARD'S NODES

- **Congenital abnormalities in joint alignment.** When joints are not aligned properly from birth, the joints can wear irregularly, leading to OA. Recent studies show that OA of the knee is more common in people with bowed legs or knock knees. People born with shallow hip sockets are likely to develop OA of the hip later in life.
- **Joint injuries that compromise the integrity of the joint.** Like congenital abnormalities, joint injuries that alter joint alignment or stability can lead to irregular wear and osteoarthritis.
- **Overuse of a particular joint.** Excessive use can lead to cartilage wear and OA.
- **Obesity.** The more weight you carry, the larger the load your joints have to support. Excessive weight is recognized as a major risk factor for the development and worsening of osteoarthritis of the knee and probably the hip.

RHEUMATOID ARTHRITIS

The second most common form of arthritis, rheumatoid arthritis (RA), affects between one and three people in every hundred. Although it can occur in people of any age, most cases are diagnosed in people between the ages of 30 and 50. Rheumatoid arthritis also affects an estimated 12,000 children. (For more information on arthritis in children, see the discussion of juvenile arthritis on the next page.)

The pain of RA is caused by inflammation of the synovium, the thin membrane that lines the joint. Inflammation can be so severe that it damages cartilage, bone and connective tissue.

If you have rheumatoid arthritis, your joints are probably affected in a symmetrical fashion. That is, if one elbow or knee is inflamed and painful, the other elbow or knee probably will be too. The joints RA is most likely to affect are those of the fingers, hands, wrists, elbows, shoulders, knees, ankles and feet.

Although no one fully understands RA, generally it is believed to be an *autoimmune disease*. In autoimmune diseases, the body's immune system, which is designed to protect us from such harmful invaders as viruses and bacteria, mistakenly turns against healthy tissue. The joint is the main site of this attack, but RA can affect the entire body. For example, you may have a low-grade fever and experience fatigue and general achiness. In rare cases, RA can affect the skin, muscles and internal organs, such as the heart and lungs.

What causes the immune system to attack healthy tissues is unknown, but scientists suspect an interplay of genetic and environmental factors may be to blame. One genetic marker, HLA-DR4, has been associated with RA development and severity.

Environmental factors suspected of playing a role in the disease include viral or bacterial infections, coffee and cigarette smoke. A recent study showed that older women who smoked were more than twice as likely to have RA as those who never smoked, and other studies have linked smoking to RA severity. A large Finnish study showed that people who drank four or more cups of coffee daily were twice as likely to have *rheumatoid factor*, an antibody associated with rheumatoid arthritis.

Because RA is approximately three times more common in women than in men, scientists believe that female hormones may also play a role. Interestingly, the use of birth control pills has been shown to offer some protection against the disease. Furthermore, during pregnancy, women who have RA often experience remissions or decreased disease activity. Researchers are trying to better understand the connection between genes, hormones and other factors that play a role in RA. The hope is that a better understanding of these factors will lead to better treatments and, eventually, ways to prevent and cure the disease.

JUVENILE ARTHRITIS

When arthritis begins before age 16, it is classified as juvenile arthritis. Although children can have almost any form of arthritis that adults can have, the most common form in children is juvenile idiopathic arthritis (JIA), which is further categorized as pauciarticular (affecting four or fewer joints), polyarticular (affecting five or more joints) and systemic (affecting the entire body).

Depending on the type, JIA may be relatively mild, or it can be progressive and disabling; it may be limited to the joints or affect the eyes and other organs. In some cases, JIA resolves by adulthood; in others, its effects are lifelong, requiring ongoing medical care. The number of cases of JIA in the UK is estimated be about 12,000.

FIBROMYALGIA

The most common arthritis-related condition, fibromyalgia, affects around 11 per cent of the population, most of them women. Unlike most conditions you'll read about in this book, fibromyalgia does not affect the joints. Instead, fibromyalgia is characterized by widespread pain and fatigue that can be debilitating.

Another common characteristic of fibromyalgia is the presence of *tender points*, or specific areas of the body that are particularly painful upon application of the slightest pressure. Because fibromyalgia can make you feel generally bad all over, many people don't

even realize they have these tender points until a doctor presses on them during a physical examination. Yet, tender points are so common in people with fibromyalgia that they are among the primary criteria doctors use to diagnose the condition. (For more information about tender points, see Chapter 3, 'Diagnosing Arthritis.')

If you have fibromyalgia, you may feel as if you have a never-ending case of the flu or as though you haven't slept for weeks. In fact, you may not have slept – at least, not well. Up to 85 per cent of people with fibromyalgia experience problems with sleep. They may fall asleep without difficulty, but they sleep lightly and wake up frequently throughout the night. They often wake up feeling tired, even after sleeping all night.

Other problems associated with fibromyalgia include headaches; difficulty in concentrating; frequent constipation or diarrhoea, or a combination of the two in conjunction with abdominal pain (a condition known as irritable bowel syndrome); bladder spasms or bladder irritability or urgency (which make you feel as though you always need to go to the toilet or that you must go immediately); and pain or dysfunction with the temporomandibular joints (TMJ), which attach the lower jaw to the skull on each side of the face.

Although the cause of fibromyalgia is not known, scientists suspect that several factors – including infectious illness, physical or emotional trauma or hormonal changes, alone or in combination – may contribute to the generalized pain, fatigue and sleep disturbances that characterize the condition. Some studies have suggested that people with fibromyalgia have abnormal levels of several chemicals that help transmit and amplify pain signals to and from the brain.

Whether these abnormalities are a cause or result of fibromyalgia is unknown. Because of the prevalence of this condition and the lack of understanding about its causes and optimal treatment, fibromyalgia has become the subject of increased research focus in recent years.

ANKYLOSING SPONDYLITIS

Ankylosing spondylitis (AS) is one of a group of diseases collectively referred to as the *spondyloarthropathies*, a term that means arthritis that affects the spine. In addition to AS, which affects about 20,000 people in the UK, this group of inflammatory diseases includes reactive arthritis, psoriatic arthritis and arthritis with inflammatory bowel disease.

The most obvious common characteristic of the spondyloarthropathies, from which they get the name, is their similar effects on the spine. Typically, these diseases attack the *sacroiliac joints* that attach the spine to the pelvis and the stack of bones called vertebrae, which form the spinal column. Other common features include an association between the diseases and a genetic type called HLA-B27; the presence of arthritis in other joints (commonly, the shoulders, hips, knees and ankles); and occasional involvement of other tissues, including those of the skin, eyes, bowel and genitourinary tract.

Traditionally, ankylosing spondylitis was thought to be primarily a disease of young men. Now, doctors have begun to realize that AS also affects women – perhaps as often as it does men. However, AS may appear differently in women, and in women its effects usually are less severe.

If you have ankylosing spondylitis, your symptoms probably began gradually, with lower back pain that you may first have noted at night in bed. As in other forms of arthritis, however, the symptoms can vary greatly from person to person. In some people, AS first shows up as pain or inflammation in such joints as a knee or hip.

In the most severe and advanced cases of AS, the tissues that support the spine can become ossified, or bone-like. When the tissues ossify, the spine may stiffen and fuse in one position, causing the body to lock in a stooped or rigid, upright position. A similar process of ossification in the ligaments that attach the ribs to the spine may make breathing difficult. In some people, AS may affect the eyes, heart and lungs. In the vast majority of people, however, fusion and organ involvement never occur.

Although no one is certain what causes ankylosing spondylitis, the finding of HLA-B27 in most people with the disease leads scientists to believe that there is an inherited component. However, because many people without the disease also have the gene, something else must be involved, such as an environmental factor that triggers the disease in susceptible people. Research in recent years has suggested that normal bowel bacteria may trigger the disease in people who are genetically predisposed to it. Other research is likely to uncover other possible triggers, as well as better ways to treat or even halt the disease.

GOUT

If you go to bed fine and wake up with excruciating pain in a single joint, typically the big toe, you probably have gout, a disease that affects about 250,000 people in the UK, mostly men aged 40–60.

Primarily a disease of men, gout is rarely seen in women before the menopause. Gout occurs when a bodily waste product called uric acid builds up in the body. Normally, excess uric acid is filtered out by the kidneys. When the kidneys don't eliminate uric acid efficiently, or when the body produces too much of it, the acid can crystallize in joints, causing pain and inflammation.

Gout usually strikes a single joint suddenly. Inflammation and swelling of the affected joint may be so severe that the skin over the joint is pulled taut and appears shiny and red or purplish. Typically, inflammation subsides on its own within a week or so. However, unless the high level of uric acid is treated, attacks will return with increasing frequency and affect more joints, including the feet, knees and elbows. If allowed to progress, gout can lead to joint damage.

Fortunately, gout is well understood, treatable and preventable. Appropriate treatment can reduce the frequency and severity of attacks and may prevent future attacks. (See 'The Gout Exception,' on page 138.)

LUPUS

Systemic lupus erythematosus (SLE), often referred to simply as lupus, is an inflammatory disease that affects about 10,000 people in the UK, considerably more women than men. It is most likely to begin during a woman's child-bearing years.

Like other forms of arthritis, lupus causes inflammation of the joints, typically those of the hands, wrists, elbows, knees and feet. Because it is a systemic disease, it also can affect the skin, blood, lungs, kidneys and cardiovascular and nervous systems.

If you have lupus, the first symptoms you notice may include fatigue, fever, achiness, weight loss, swollen glands, skin rashes (especially over the cheeks and bridge of the nose) and pain in the joints, chest and abdomen.

Over time, you may experience other signs and symptoms, such as a sensitivity to sunlight that causes rashes after minimal sun exposure; sores on the tongue, inside the mouth and in the nose; chest pain; shortness of breath; swelling of the legs and feet; blanching of the fingers in response to cold temperatures or stress; and dry eyes and mouth.

As the disease progresses, you may experience periods when the disease becomes more active (a flare) or becomes less active or inactive (a remission). On rare occasions, a person may have a complete or long-lasting remission. Like most other forms of arthritis, lupus is chronic, meaning that it lasts a long time – usually a lifetime. However, in most people, lupus becomes less active with age.

Although no one is certain what causes lupus, like rheumatoid arthritis, it is considered to be an autoimmune disease. Scientists suspect that certain genes, and perhaps a combination of different genes, predispose people to develop lupus. Genes alone do not determine who will get lupus. Even in genetically susceptible people, some environmental factor, such as an infection, may trigger the disease. Female hormones are believed to play a significant role in lupus.

Research work continues to improve both the understanding of lupus and its treatment. Major participants in the UK are Lupus UK, a self-help support group that offers advice to people with lupus as well as raising funds for research, and the St Thomas' Lupus Trust, which supports research into the condition as well as providing support and information to professionals and to people who have the condition. In the USA there is the Alliance for Lupus Research (a non-profit partnership involving the Arthritis Foundation and a private individual).

BACK PAIN

At some point in their lives, an estimated two-thirds of adults will experience some type of low back pain. The cause may be a day of strenuous activity, an injury suffered in an automobile accident, or a single episode of bending improperly to lift a heavy load.

For some, however, the low back pain is caused by arthritis of the spine. The most common cause of chronic back pain is osteoarthritis. Other arthritis-related causes of

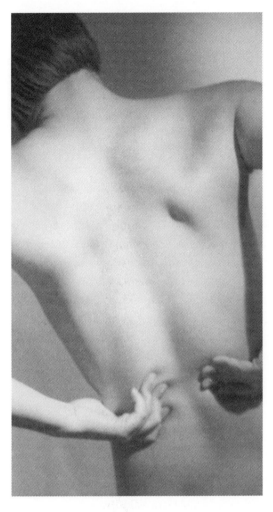

persists in some people and not others, offers hope for easing or even preventing this common problem. For many people, back pain goes away on its own, with time, regardless of treatment. For others, back pain requires treatment that is targeted to the problem causing the pain.

OTHER RELATED DISEASES

The conditions we have just described are some of the more common diseases that fall into the category of arthritis and related conditions. But there are many other conditions related to arthritis. Some of these conditions may occur in conjunction with other major forms of arthritis, such as rheumatoid arthritis or lupus. These diseases include the following.

Osteoporosis

The most common disorder of the bone, osteoporosis (or porous bones) is a condition in which the body loses so much bone mass that bones are susceptible to disabling fractures after the slightest trauma. The disease is most common in older women, whose bodies no longer produce large levels of the bone-preserving hormone oestrogen.

Some medications used to treat inflammatory forms of arthritis, including such corticosteroids as prednisone, can increase the risk of developing osteoporosis.

Osteoporosis is not painful. In fact, it's likely that you might never experience symptoms until you suffer a broken bone. Fortunately, the condition can be treated to

back pain include nerves that are compressed or pinched due to bony overgrowth of the spine; fracture or compression of the vertebrae (the bones that make up the spine) due to osteoporosis; and slipped or ruptured disks (the wedges of cartilage that provide cushion between the vertebrae).

Research examining the causes of back pain, who is likely to have it, and why it minimize fracture risk. (See 'Nutrition for Healthy Bones', page 71.)

Polymyositis

Polymyositis, an inflammation of many muscles, is a disease of generalized weakness that results from inflammation of the muscles, primarily those of the shoulders, upper arms, thighs and hips. Weakness may develop gradually, over the course of months or years, or it can happen suddenly. In some people, polymyositis affects the muscles in the throat or chest, leading to difficulties with swallowing or breathing.

When polymyositis is accompanied by a patchy rash, typically seen over the eyelids, upper chest, neck or hands, doctors refer to the disease as *dermatomyositis*.

Like many arthritis-related diseases, polymyositis is more common in women than in men, and its development is linked to genetic and environmental factors. Polymyositis occurs most often between the ages of 30 and 60.

Scleroderma

Translated literally as 'hard skin,' scleroderma results from an abnormal overgrowth of collagen within the skin, in a process called fibrosis. In some forms of the disease, the effects of this abnormal overgrowth are limited to the skin and underlying tissues. In others, however, connective-tissue buildup can affect the function of the joints, blood vessels and internal organs, such as the heart, lungs, kidneys and intestines.

Polymyalgia Rheumatica

Although this term means pain in many muscles, polymyalgia rheumatica (PMR) is actually a disease of the joints. Inflammation in the joints of neck, shoulder and hip areas causes stiffness and aching in those areas. PMR affects about 1 person in 1,000, and approximately 66 per cent of them are women. The disease rarely occurs in people before age 50; the average age at which PMR begins is 70.

Sjögren's Syndrome

A condition that affects about 500,000 people in the UK, 90 per cent of whom are women, Sjögren's syndrome is an autoimmune disease that may occur on its own or in conjunction with another disease, such as rheumatoid arthritis, lupus or scleroderma. In people with Sjögren's syndrome, a type of white blood cell called a lymphocyte invades moisture-producing glands, causing inflammation and such problems as dry mouth and eyes.

In addition to tissue dryness, Sjögren's syndrome can cause inflammation in the joints, lungs, kidneys, nerves, thyroid gland and skin.

Reactive Arthritis

Sometimes called infectious arthritis, reactive arthritis is caused by infection, typically by a bacterium, such as staphylococcus (staph), or a virus, such as hepatitis C. Less commonly, the infection results from a fungus, such as *Blastomyces* or *Candida*.

Signs of recative arthritis differ by the severity of the condition and the type of infection involved. Bacterial infections, for example, most often affect a single joint, typically a large joint, such as the knee. Symptoms of bacterial arthritis include moderate to severe joint pain, swelling, redness and warmth. Such symptoms often come on quickly and may be accompanied by fever and chills. The symptoms of viral-related arthritis depend largely on the particular virus involved. Most types of viral-related arthritis develop gradually and cause widespread joint aches, rather than arthritis in one or a few joints. Fungal infections are usually insidious, with only mild inflammation, but occasionally, fungal infection can cause an acute arthritis in a single joint.

Reactive arthritis can occur in people of any age, but about half of the cases affect people over age 60. Risk factors include having a coexisting disease, such as RA, another inflammatory form of arthritis, diabetes mellitus, chronic liver disease or any condition in which the immune system is suppressed.

Psoriatic Arthritis

As the name suggests, psoriatic arthritis is a form of joint disease accompanied by psoriasis, a disease of the skin that is characterized by thickened, inflamed patches of skin covered by silver-grey scales.

In the majority of people with psoriatic arthritis, the skin disease precedes arthritis by several months or even years. In rare cases, arthritis precedes the skin disease. Psoriatic arthritis affects men and women in equal numbers and generally begins in people between the ages of 30 and 50. In addition to the joints and skin, psoriatic arthritis may affect the nails, causing thickening, pitting and separation from the nail bed.

Osteonecrosis

Also referred to as avascular necrosis, osteonecrosis (literally 'bone death') typically affects a segment of the bone and cartilage of the joint, leading to pain and, eventually, loss of movement of the joint. The condition is most common in people between the ages of 30 and 60 and can occur as a complication of corticosteroid therapy for arthritis or for an injury to the joint.

The most common sites of osteonecrosis are the hip and the knee, but it can develop in any joint. Severe damage to the joint may require a total joint replacement.

Raynaud's Phenomenon

Raynaud's phenomenon is a condition in which the small blood vessels of the hands and feet contract and go into spasms in response to cold or stress. As the vessels contract, the hands or feet turn white and cold, and then blue. As the vessels open and blood flow returns, the hands and feet become red. In severe cases, the tissues in the tips of the fingers and toes may be damaged. Sometimes, Raynaud's phenomenon is associated with an underlying autoimmune disease, such as lupus or scleroderma. It commonly occurs in the absence of arthritis.

Carpal Tunnel Syndrome

Carpal tunnel syndrome occurs when the median nerve, which supplies the thumb side of the hand with sensation, becomes compressed within the wrist. The resulting symptoms can include tingling, numbness and pain in the thumb and the first and middle fingers; shooting pain from the hand, along the arm, to the shoulder; and a swollen feeling in the fingers.

The carpal tunnel, an opening in the bones of the wrist through which the median nerve runs, is narrow, and any swelling or inflammation of the connective tissue that holds together the bones of the wrist can cause pressure on the nerve or irritate it. Causes of inflammation can include injuries to the wrist or forearm, arthritis and activities that require repetitive finger or wrist motion.

Spinal Stenosis

Literally meaning spinal narrowing, spinal stenosis is a condition that occurs when bony overgrowths in the spinal column cause the column to narrow and press on the nerves housed within. Because these nerves have many functions, the condition may cause diverse problems in the lower body, including low back pain, pain or numbness in the legs, constipation and urinary incontinence.

Vasculitis

Vasculitis is an inflammation of the blood vessels that can occur with rheumatoid arthritis and some other inflammatory forms of arthritis. There are many types of vasculitis.

The location and effects of vasculitis depend largely on which vessels are affected. In RA, for example, the vessels affected are often those that supply the skin and supporting nerves. The result may be skin ulceration.

In a condition called temporal arteritis, the vessel affected is the artery that supplies the head and scalp. If untreated, temporal arteritis can lead to vision problems and even permanent loss of vision.

UNDERSTANDING WHICH FORM OF ARTHRITIS YOU HAVE

As evident from their descriptions, many forms of arthritis and related conditions share common symptoms. Other diseases may also share the similar symptoms of arthritis, making it impossible to determine on your own which condition you have. Gauging the disease's severity also can be difficult. Some people with severe arthritis report relatively mild pain, while others who have relatively mild arthritis report having severe pain.

Because the specific condition and its severity will largely dictate the treatment you need, it's important to see a doctor for a diagnosis. The following chapter looks at some of the signs that indicate it is time to see a doctor about your joint pain, and it discusses methods your doctor may use to determine which form of arthritis or related condition you have.

Diagnosing Arthritis

3

CHAPTER 3: DIAGNOSING ARTHRITIS

Joint and muscle pain can have many causes, some of which are not serious and will resolve with or without treatment. At other times, arthritis can signal a serious problem that requires prompt medical attention to keep it from getting worse. Obviously, it's important to know the difference!

In general, you should consult your doctor if you experience arthritis symptoms that come on suddenly, such as a joint rapidly becoming hot, swollen or difficult to move, or if you have any of the following signs for longer than two weeks:

- Pain in a joint that doesn't go away or keeps returning
- Joint stiffness
- Swelling in a joint, especially with warmth and redness
- Joint or muscle pain accompanied by fatigue, malaise or fever

The first step of a medical evaluation for arthritis will probably be to see your GP. If your GP doesn't feel confident about diagnosing or treating your condition, or if you or your GP suspect a condition that requires specialized knowledge and care, you should see a rheumatologist. A rheumatologist is a doctor who specializes in the diagnosis and treatment of arthritis and related diseases.

Regardless of what kind of doctor you see, the initial evaluation probably will include a physical examination and a medical history.

THE MEDICAL HISTORY AND THE EXAMINATION

For the medical history, your doctor will ask you about any symptoms, past injuries or illnesses and lifestyle habits, such as smoking, that may be associated with arthritis. Because certain forms of arthritis seem to have a genetic basis, you can expect questions about family members' illnesses, particularly auto-immune and musculoskeletal problems. It's best to become familiar with your family history, if possible, and make notes about any concerns you have before you see the doctor. (For some idea of the type of information you should bring to your first appointment, see 'What to Tell Your Doctor' on the next page.)

The physical examination will vary depending on the symptoms you have. Your doctor may visually examine, feel and move your joints, and examine your skin, mouth and eyes to check for evidence of a particular form of arthritis.

You will probably be asked to walk, raise your arms and bend over, so the doctor can observe your gait and flexibility. He or she may apply pressure to certain points on your body (including points at the base of the skull and around the shoulders, thighs and inner knees) called tender points, which are painful in people with fibromyalgia. (See 'The Fibromyalgia Examination' on page 35.)

In many cases, a doctor who is knowledgeable about the various forms of arthritis and their signs and symptoms can get a pretty

What To Tell Your Doctor

Thinking about your concerns and writing them down to bring with you when you see your doctor is a handy way to make sure that everything important is discussed. Think about these points before your appointment:

- When the pain started
- What the pain feels like
- How long the pain lasts
- What time of day the pain is worst
- Other symptoms you've noticed
- Other medical conditions you have
- Childhood illnesses you've had
- Adult illnesses you've had
- Operations you've had
- Injuries you've had
- Lifestyle habits (bad and good)
- Medical conditions your family members have had

good idea of the type of arthritis you have from the examination and medical history.

In some cases, your doctor will order or perform medical tests that may provide clues to what's going on in your body and help make a diagnosis or to confirm what they already suspect. The following types of tests may be used to help make or confirm a diagnosis.

Laboratory Tests

Most lab tests require no more than drawing a small amount of blood or providing a urine sample, but can provide valuable clues to what's occurring elsewhere in the body. Here are some of the most common lab tests.

Erythrocyte Sedimentation Rate. Also referred to as ESR or 'sed rate', this blood test measures how fast red blood cells fall to the bottom of a test tube. Because inflammatory substances in the blood make red blood cells cling together and because the clumps that form are heavier and fall faster than single cells, a high ESR can signal inflammation. The higher the ESR, the greater the inflammation. Most inflammatory diseases, including rheumatoid arthritis, ankylosing spondylitis, vasculitis, juvenile arthritis and polymyalgia rheumatica, are characterized by a high ESR.

C-reactive Protein. C-reactive protein appears in the blood during inflammatory processes and thus may be useful in determining if you have an inflammatory form of arthritis. Some doctors use the C-reactive protein test instead of or in conjunction with the erythrocyte sedimentation rate (ESR) to monitor the progress of arthritis.

Full Blood Count (FBC). The FBC is made up of measurements of specific blood components, which can help your doctor diagnose disease and monitor the effects of disease and its treatment. Findings of an FBC might include anaemia, which would indicate chronic inflammation, blood loss or perhaps the presence of inflammatory bowel disease; low white-blood cell count, which might indicate lupus; high white-blood cell count, which could indicate infection or systemic JIA; or low blood platelets, which could indicate lupus.

Uric Acid. Abnormally high levels of the bodily waste product uric acid in the blood may indicate gout, a condition in which excess uric acid is deposited as crystals in the joints and other tissues (see Chapter 2). To confirm a diagnosis of gout, however, your doctor will need to examine the joint fluid for uric acid crystals.

Urinalysis. Urinalysis refers to a battery of tests used to screen for urinary tract infections, kidney disease and other health problems that can cause changes in the urine. In people with lupus, urinalysis may be used to check for protein and red blood cells, which can indicate kidney inflammation, a condition referred to as lupus nephritis.

Rheumatoid Factor (RF) Test (or RA latex test). The presence of rheumatoid factor (RF), an autoantibody that is produced in large amounts in people with rheumatoid arthritis, can help a doctor diagnose that disease. Approximately 80 per cent of people with RA test positive for rheumatoid factor. However, because a smaller percentage of people without RA also test positive, the presence of RF in the blood doesn't confirm a diagnosis.

Antinuclear Antibody (ANA). Antinuclear antibodies are antibodies directed against the nuclei, or command centres, of the body's cells. ANAs can be found in approximately 95 per cent of people with lupus. These antibodies also can be found in many other forms of arthritis, including rheumatoid arthritis, scleroderma, polymyositis and Sjögren's syndrome, and they are sometimes found in low amounts (called 'low titres') in healthy people. Used in conjunction with other tests, ANA can help diagnose these diseases.

Anti-DNA. Antibodies to DNA (deoxyribonucleic acid, the hereditary material in the nucleus of every cell) are common in people with lupus. Because these antibodies are rarely found in people with any other disease, the finding of anti-DNA antibodies in the blood is used to diagnose lupus.

Complement. When antibodies combine with invading agents, a substance in the blood called *complement* aids the body's immune defences. Blood samples showing low levels of complement can suggest such inflammatory conditions as lupus or vasculitis. Other tests are necessary, however, to aid in the diagnosis of these diseases.

Joint Fluid Examination. The examination of fluid withdrawn from the joint cavity can help your doctor diagnose gout or infectious arthritis. In gout, crystals of uric acid – a bodily waste product – can be found in the joint fluid. The finding of bacteria in the joint fluid indicates reactive arthritis.

Lyme Serology. To confirm a diagnosis of Lyme disease, blood is tested for antibodies that are made in response to *Borrelia burgdorferi*, the spirochaete (spiral-shaped bacterium) that causes the disease.

Tissue Typing. The finding of a specific genetic marker called HLA-B27 in the blood through tissue typing helps confirm a diagnosis of ankylosing spondylitis, a form of arthritis that primarily affects the spine and sacroiliac joints, or reactive arthritis, a similar disease that is characterized by inflammation of the joints, eyes and urethra. The finding of a marker called HLA-DR4 may indicate RA.

Imaging Tests

Imaging studies are used to view components of the body to detect and assess signs of arthritis. Your doctor may order one of the following radiological tests.

X-rays. Plain X-rays are often used in the diagnosis of arthritis because they enable the doctor to view the bony structures that make up the joint. X-rays can show such problems as fluid accumulation in the joint, cartilage damage, patterns of cartilage wear and abnormalities of bone. These signs can help doctors determine which form of arthritis you have.

In osteoarthritis, the joint space (the area between the two bones that make up the joint) may look narrow and uneven because of the irregular wear and damage that OA causes to the cartilage. The ends of the bones may look dense, and there may be evidence of bony growths called spurs. Rheumatoid arthritis, on the other hand, causes more consistent joint-space narrowing. X-rays may show bone thinning around the joint or bone erosion.

X-rays also show certain bony changes in the spine, which helps doctors diagnose ankylosing spondylitis and other spondyloarthropathies. Other forms of arthritis, such as psoriatic arthritis, also show characteristic patterns of joint damage on X-rays, enabling doctors to differentiate them.

Sometimes a doctor will inject dye into a joint before X-raying it, a procedure called arthrography. The dye helps highlight the spaces inside the joints and enables your doctor to view and diagnose such problems as damage to the cartilage, supporting muscles, tendons and ligaments.

DEXA scans. Dual energy X-ray absorptiometry (DEXA) scans are the most reliable way to diagnose osteoporosis and determine a person's risk for a bone fracture.

A DEXA scan is similar to an X-ray, except that it uses much less radiation. Having a DEXA scan involves lying on a table while an imaging machine passes over you, measuring bone density at the hip and spine. The procedure is painless and usually takes 15 to 20 minutes.

Because osteoporosis is such a common and potentially dangerous problem for women who are past the menopause, some doctors recommend a routine DEXA scan for all women five to ten years after the menopause. If you have an inflammatory disease, such as RA or lupus, your doctor may order a DEXA scan regardless of your age, particularly if you take a corticosteroid medication for the disease.

MRI. Magnetic resonance imaging (MRI) is a procedure in which a very strong magnet passes a force through the body to create a clear, detailed image of a cross-section of the body. The procedure is harmless and does not expose the body to radiation.

The advantage of MRI scans over plain X-rays is that MRI provides detailed images of such soft-tissue structures as the synovium, tendons, ligaments and muscles, as well as bone.

Arthritis-related uses for MRI include diagnosing avascular necrosis of the hip; ankylosing spondylitis, spinal stenosis and other back-related problems; injuries to the soft tissues of the knee; and, less commonly, other types of joint problems.

Having an MRI typically involves lying on a long, narrow table that slides into a large, tunnel-like tube within the scanner. Several images are taken of the joint or organ being examined. Each image takes between 2 and 15 minutes; the entire procedure takes about an hour.

In the past, people who were claustrophobic were not good candidates for MRI because the procedure requires being confined in a small space. In recent years, however, a type of machine called open MRI has been introduced that is less confining than traditional models. Although the images these newer machines produce may not be of the same quality as those produced by traditional machines, they do make MRI an option for more people.

If you wear a pacemaker or have any type of metal implant in your body (including implants for orthopaedic reasons) either type of MRI may be inappropriate for you. If you have concerns about MRI, it's best to discuss them with your doctor beforehand.

Ultrasonography. Increasingly, doctors are using ultrasonography – the use of sound waves to produce pictures of structures within the body – in the diagnosis of arthritis and related diseases. Benefits of ultrasonography, often referred to as ultrasound, are that it doesn't use radiation and it can take pictures of the body's soft tissues.

Ultrasound can be useful in the diagnosis of such problems as bursitis, an inflammation of the bursae that cushion bony points such as the shoulder, and plantar fasciitis, inflammation of the tissues under the heel bone. Doctors also use ultrasonography to assess inflammation of the synovium, the membrane that lines the joint, and to detect the presence of fluid within the joint cavity.

Biopsies

Biopsies are tests performed on pieces of bodily tissue that are removed surgically, most often through small incisions. Depending on the piece of tissue examined, your doctor may use a biopsy to diagnose diseases of the joint, muscle, skin or blood vessels. Below are descriptions of biopsies often used to diagnose arthritis and related diseases.

Muscle. Used in the diagnosis of polymyositis or dermatomyositis, a muscle biopsy involves removing a sample of muscle, usually from the thigh, through a small incision.

Skin. Used to diagnose or confirm a diagnosis of lupus or vasculitis, a skin biopsy is obtained with a special needle inserted into the skin. The tissue is usually taken from an area where a small scar would not be very noticeable.

Synovium. Biopsy of the synovium (the joint lining) can help diagnose various forms of arthritis. To remove a sample of the synovium, your doctor will insert a special biopsy needle into the joint. A synovial biopsy can also be obtained by a procedure called arthroscopy, which is discussed later in this section.

Temporal artery. Temporal artery biopsy is performed to help diagnose giant cell arteritis (GCA), also called temporal arteritis. The procedure involves making an inch-long vertical incision in front of the ear and removing a small segment of the temporal artery for examination.

Kidney. Kidney biopsy involves inserting a special needle through an incision in the lower back and removing a small sample of kidney for examination. If you have lupus, and urinalysis shows evidence of kidney inflammation, a kidney biopsy can be used to confirm a diagnosis of lupus nephritis.

Arthroscopy

Doctors sometimes use a surgical procedure called arthroscopy to diagnose or evaluate joint problems. In arthroscopy, a thin tube with a light at the end, called an arthroscope, is inserted directly into the joint through a small incision. The arthroscope, which is attached to a closed-circuit television, illuminates the interior of the joint and enables your doctor to see it on the screen.

The procedure typically is performed under local or spinal anaesthesia on an outpatient basis. If a problem is detected through arthroscopy, the damage can often be repaired during the same procedure.

Although the use of arthroscopy is far from routine in the diagnosis of arthritis-related problems, it is commonly used to remove loose pieces of tissue that cause pain, repair torn cartilage, or smooth rough joint surfaces. Arthroscopy is sometimes used for more extensive surgery, such as ligament reconstruction and *synovectomy*, the removal of a diseased joint lining. For more information about arthroscopy, see Chapter 8.

Diagnosis Difficulties

Some arthritis-related diseases are fairly rare. A doctor who doesn't specialize in arthritis treatment, such as a GP, may never have seen a patient with that particular disease and may have difficulty diagnosing it. Even for a specialized doctor, arriving at a precise diagnosis can take time. Here, we will look at some of the reasons why this occurs.

- **Same symptoms, different diseases.** Some forms of arthritis share characteristics with one another or with unrelated diseases. For example, joint pain and inflammation can be a symptom of many diseases. Without diagnostic tests, it may be difficult to differentiate between RA and ankylosing spondylitis or between RA and gout. Raynaud's phenomenon, a condition in which the fingers blanch in response to cold temperatures or emotional stress (see Chapter 2), may rarely be an early symptom of both lupus and scleroderma.

- **Same person, different diseases.** Because a person can have more than one form of arthritis simultaneously, sorting through which condition is causing what problem may take some time. For example, a person with lupus may have hip pain that is caused by osteonecrosis. A person with RA may have a swollen knee due to reactive arthritis.

- **Disease evolution.** Some forms of arthritis can take months or years to completely reveal themselves. Blood tests that once were negative may, when repeated, become positive. A pattern of joint involvement or other symptoms may become more pronounced or clearer. Some forms of arthritis that accompany viral infections can mimic RA or other conditions, but resolve on their own, usually after a few weeks.

The diagnosis process may not occur quickly or exactly as you would hope or expect. In most cases, however, your doctor can give you a pretty good idea of what's going on, even if a precise diagnosis takes some time.

Treatment will probably depend on the particular form of arthritis or related condition you have, but a precise diagnosis often is not essential before beginning treatment. What's most important early on is that you are being seen by a doctor who can help minimize the symptoms of your condition. Perhaps your doctor will give you a medication that will keep your condition from worsening or causing irreparable joint or organ damage.

THE FIBROMYALGIA EXAMINATION

For many forms of arthritis and related conditions, positive results on certain lab tests can help a doctor make or confirm a diagnosis. For fibromyalgia, however, there are no routine lab tests to confirm or rule out the condition. In diagnosing fibromyalgia, the history and physical exam take on added importance.

One of the key determinants of a fibromyalgia diagnosis is the presence of tender points, which are tender, painful areas in the muscles, tendons or other areas of the body where the bone can be felt through the skin. Many people with fibromyalgia don't even realize they have tender points until the doctor applies pressure to them.

The location of these tender points is fairly consistent from person to person. There are 18 recognized tender points in fibromyalgia. In general, to be diagnosed with fibromyalgia, you must have at least 11 of these tender points in combination with widespread pain.

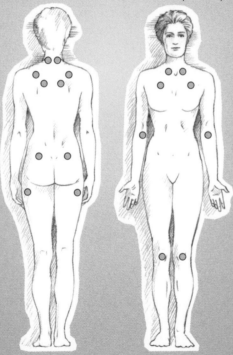

TENDER POINTS: POINTS OF THE BODY WHERE
FIBROMYALGIA PAIN IS MOST COMMON

After the Diagnosis

4

CHAPTER 4: AFTER THE DIAGNOSIS

Getting a diagnosis can bring mixed emotions. It can be upsetting and frightening to learn that you have a chronic disease – that your problem may be more serious than 'aches and pains'. However, you may feel a sense of relief to have a name for what has been troubling you. Regardless of the way your diagnosis affects you emotionally, try to remember that a diagnosis is a positive step. It allows you to learn more about your specific medical condition and what you and your doctor can do to help you get better.

GETTING PROPER CARE – A TEAM EFFORT

If you have been seeing your GP up to the point of your diagnosis, you may be referred to or may ask to see a rheumatologist or orthopaedic surgeon, depending on the diagnosis. Rheumatologists are doctors who specialize in treating arthritis and related conditions. Orthopaedic surgeons treat diseases of the bone and joints surgically.

Although most cases of osteoarthritis may be treated quite effectively by a GP or family doctor, diseases such as lupus and RA may require the knowledge and experience of a specialist.

If your GP feels that you should see a rheumatologist, he or she will refer you to one at your local hospital. Although at your first appointment you may well be seen by the consultant rheumatologist, on subsequent vis-

its you might be seen by another doctor on that consultant's team. Whoever you see, though, will be working under the direction of the consultant.

Members of Your Health-Care Team

At some point you may be referred by your GP to another health professional, including a specialist at your local hospital, to help you manage the various aspects of your disease. In addition to a rheumatologist or an orthopaedic surgeon, the people who may be part of your health-care team include the following professionals.

Other doctors. Because different forms of arthritis can be systemic, meaning that they affect the entire body, your care may involve seeing doctors who specialize in treating organs and systems affected by arthritis-related disease. In addition to rheumatologists and orthopaedic surgeons, these doctors may include dermatologists, who specialize in treating problems of the skin, hair and nails; ophthalmologists, who specialize in problems of the eyes; nephrologists, who specialize in kidney disease; geriatricians, who specialize in the treatment of older people; and paediatric rheumatologists, who specialize in treating arthritis in children.

Not all of these people will necessarily be available to you through the NHS – for

WORKING WITH YOUR DOCTOR: FINDING THE RIGHT FIT

Managing your arthritis requires a team effort. But what if your doctor doesn't want you to be a part of the team? Many doctors appreciate informed, involved patients, but there are exceptions.

Some doctors view a patient's questions as a sign of distrust or are put off by patients who want to take charge of their own health care. For some patients, such doctors are fine. Just as there are doctors who want you to follow their orders – full stop – there are patients who prefer to put all of their medical decisions in the hands of the doctor. These patients find comfort in knowing that someone else is in charge.

While the best doctor–patient relationship is one in which there is some give-and-take, what's most important is that you see eye-to-eye with your doctor. Problems arise when there is a discrepancy between the way you and your doctor prefer to work. If you want to take a role in your health care, but your doctor expects you to follow orders without question, it may be time to find a new doctor.

Before you switch, however, be sure that you're not asking for or expecting too much. Although your doctor should be willing to answer questions and be open to the possibility of different treatments you would like to try, no doctor has the time to answer endless lists of queries from every patient.

A doctor who merely agrees with everything you suggest is not good for you. And prescribing or condoning every treatment you mention can be downright dangerous.

example, massage therapists or acupuncturists. Moreover, some NHS services, such as chiropody/podiatry, can be in short supply, resulting in a long wait to be seen.

Physiotherapist. If arthritis causes pain and limited motion in your joints, or causes difficulties with walking, stretching, bending or climbing stairs, a physiotherapist (physio) may help. A physio can devise an exercise plan that strengthens your muscles and increases your range of motion. Physios also prescribe such devices as canes, splints or shoe inserts. Many physios are trained in soft-tissue massage, which people with arthritis often find helpful to relieve pain and stiffness.

Occupational therapist. An occupational therapist (OT) can help you find ways to manage daily tasks at home and on the job. If arthritis makes it difficult to handle such tasks as cooking, typing, driving, brushing your teeth or buttoning your clothes, an OT may suggest different ways to do these tasks or arrange for assistive devices or splints.

Nurses. In addition to taking your blood pressure, drawing blood and providing routine care, nurses function as patient educators and advocates. When you visit your GP practice or health centre, you might well be seen by a practice nurse for routine matters. Practice nurses work alongside GPs, giving the GPs time to concentrate on more complex medical matters. A role being developed for experienced nurses is that of nurse practitioner; nurse practitioners will be trained further to help doctors in diagnosis, evaluating and monitoring patients, and in some cases writing prescriptions and carrying out minor surgery as well.

State registered dietitian. Diet and weight management are important in arthritis, because excess weight can add stress to fragile joints and can complicate joint surgery. A proper diet can help you reduce your risk of other health problems, such as diabetes, cardiovascular disease and some cancers. A consultation with a dietitian may help you find a healthful diet that fits your lifestyle.

Psychologist. When you're struggling with a chronic disease, it's understandable that you may get depressed. Mental-health professionals can help you deal with the psychological

aspects of your illness, such as depression, anxiety and anger.

Psychologists cannot prescribe medications. If you have a problem that requires or would be helped by medication, they will refer you to a psychiatrist. Psychiatrists are medical doctors with psychiatric training who can prescribe such medications as antidepressants.

Pharmacist. No matter which type of arthritis you have, there is a good chance that you will take some type of medication for it. Your pharmacist can be a good source of information about the medications your doctor prescribes and the medications you purchase over the counter (i.e. without a prescription). Don't hesitate to ask your pharmacist questions about side effects, how to take medication or which sorts of over-the-counter medications are appropriate for you.

Podiatrist and chiropodist. A podiatrist, or chiropodist, treats conditions of the foot, from nail infections to arthritis-damaged joints. Podiatrists are licensed to perform minor surgery. If arthritis affects your feet, a podiatrist may be a member of your health-care team.

Dentist. If Sjögren's syndrome causes dry mouth, if arthritis affects your jaw joint (a condition called temporomandibular joint disorder) or makes it difficult to perform proper oral hygiene, you're particularly vulnerable to dental problems. For that reason, it's especially important that you see a dentist regularly to detect and take care of any problems before they become severe. In addition, a dentist may offer advice on how to brush and floss your teeth if arthritis affects your hands.

Acupuncturist. If you need help with pain and are willing to try complementary therapy, you may want to see an acupuncturist. Acupuncturists insert slender needles into the skin at various points on the body to relieve pain. The theory behind acupuncture is that the practice corrects the flow of *qi*, the body's vital energy, which optimizes health. Modern research suggests that acupuncture may ease pain by causing the release of endorphins. A few acupuncturists are also doctors. Check an acupuncturist's credentials before you make your first appointment. Nowadays, some physiotherapy departments will do acupuncture

Massage therapist. You know how good it feels to have your back and shoulders rubbed when you are achy and stiff. Massage therapists are specially trained and certified to perform therapeutic massage, which can

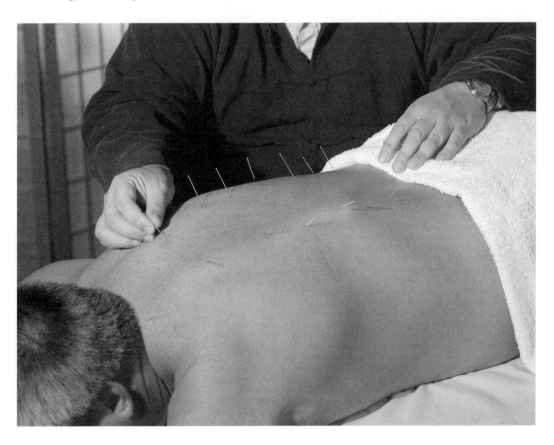

relieve muscle tension, improve range of motion and, perhaps, ease pain. You might also receive massage from a physio.

Chiropractor. Chiropractors use manual manipulation of the joints to increase range of motion and help relieve pain.

For people with certain types of arthritis, however, manipulations may not be indicated or safe. Chiropractors do not perform surgery or prescribe medication.

Social worker. Social workers – who work for your local authority rather than the health service – can help with the practical aspects of disease, such as assessing you for a home care assistant or for state benefits. They may also be involved in providing adaptations to your home to help with activities of daily living.

The health-care professionals you see and the treatment you receive will depend on a number of factors, including the type of arthritis you have, your symptoms and their severity, treatment preferences of you and your doctor, and your general physical condition, including any other medical problems you have and medications you take for them.

Regardless of which or how many people are on your team, it's important that you have an honest give-and-take relationship with the person, usually either your rheumatologist or your GP, who coordinates your arthritis care.

Your doctor will probably discuss lifestyle issues in addition to your medical treatment. Are you physically active or sedentary most of the time? Are you trim or overweight? Do you eat a varied diet, with plenty of fruit and vegetables? Do you smoke? All of these factors can influence your general health and your arthritis. If your doctor doesn't bring up these issues, you should. Although medication and other treatments are important in arthritis, a big part of your treatment's success has to do with you. *You* should be the leader of your health-care team.

THE IMPORTANCE OF INFORMATION – AND WHERE TO FIND IT

As the leader of your health-care team, you need to arm yourself with knowledge. Being informed enables you to talk more confidently with your doctor and other health-care professionals. It can also help you understand which symptoms need to be brought to your doctor's attention immediately and which symptoms should resolve without treatment. Being knowledgeable also makes you aware of potential treatments you can discuss with your doctors and gives you a sense of control that has been shown repeatedly in studies to improve the outcome of disease.

Although you will get much of your information from the doctor, your quest for knowledge should not stop at the doctor's surgery. Today, more than ever, information is available to help you understand and manage your disease – if you know where to look.

One of your first stops for information should be Arthritis Care. Through its publications (booklets, leaflets, *Arthritis News*

MEDICAL RESEARCH: SEPARATE FACT FROM FICTION

Today, more than ever, consumers have access to an abundance of information about arthritis and other topics. Although much of what you read may be accurate and helpful, a great deal of the information you'll find in publications and on the Internet is not. Even good, accurate information may not apply to your particular situation or your form of arthritis.

How can you separate the good from the bad, useless or dangerous? Evaluate everything you read with the following criteria:

Consider the source. Was it published in a peer-reviewed journal? The most reliable studies are those published in reputable journals, which have been reviewed by other doctors before publication. Vague references to being scientifically tested may mean nothing.

Who did the research? Was the research conducted by an institution that is familiar to you? Does the article say who funded the study? A study conducted at a major medical centre may be more reputable than one conducted by a single doctor in his private practice, although there are exceptions. Research funded by the Arthritis Research Campaign, for example, is more likely to be reliable than research funded by the manufacturer of an unfamiliar arthritis remedy. However, pharmaceutical companies sponsor much of the research into treatments for arthritis, and they play an important role in bringing new drugs to the marketplace. Your doctor should be in a good position to evaluate the credibility of a study.

Who was studied? Although the research may be solid, it may mean nothing for you if the people in the study were in a different situation from yours. In other words, a new drug that looks promising in 100 women with rheumatoid arthritis may be of no use for a man with osteoarthritis.

Have you seen similar reports elsewhere? When evaluating a report in a magazine or newspaper or on a web site, check around to see if you can find similar information elsewhere. When writing about technical medical topics, it's easy for a writer to get facts wrong. If you see consistent reports in several locations, however, the information is likely to be correct.

Is the article trying to sell you something? Be wary of articles written to promote a product or articles that use sensational claims and anecdotes rather than verifiable, scientific information.

magazine) web site and telephone helpline, Arthritis Care offers a wealth of information on many arthritis-related subjects – and much of it is free. To obtain copies, get in touch with the UK office (contact details on page 175). Arthritis Care also offers courses where you can learn to self-manage your particular condition; you will meet and talk to others who are managing problems similar to yours.

To find an Arthritis Care branch in your area, contact the UK office by phone or on its web site.

Your Health-Care Provider

In addition to your regional Arthritis Care office, your doctor, nurse, pharmacist and other health-care professionals may have handouts or leaflets on your condition. They may also be able to direct you to helpful classes, support groups or seminars, or even to another patient with your same condition who can offer firsthand advice and lend moral support.

Your Local Library

Your local library probably has a section on health and will include self-help books on a range of illnesses and conditions such as arthritis. You can take these home to read at your leisure, and find ones that are particularly helpful. Some books may be for reference only – you cannot take them away. In this case you can probably photocopy the pages that are relevant to you. One such reference book is the *Medical Directory*, which

gives individual doctors' training and special interests. Your library will also have a list of local doctors.

The library might also take a selection of magazines that contain information on a variety of health topics. Articles range from the warning signs and treatments for specific diseases to getting along with your doctor.

If you have access to a medical library, you'll have considerably more resources from which to choose, including computer databases and medical journals and textbooks. Sometimes your local library can get medical books and journals on loan from a larger library if you ask. Keep in mind that the information you will find is targeted to medical professionals. If you have difficulty understanding an article that seems interesting or relevant to you, make a photocopy or make notes to take along on your next visit to your doctor, who may be able to help you understand it.

Bookshops and Newsagents

Bookshops have a wealth of information, including books written for the general public – such as this one. There will probably be a health and self-help section for you to browse through and find one (or more) that appeals to you. If you've found that a library book was particularly useful, you can buy a copy for yourself. If you can't see the book you want, it can probably be ordered for you.

Newsagents carry a wide range of magazines, including some that concentrate on health matters. Many of the more general magazines have a section about health and will often have an article about a specific disease or disorder.

Other Voluntary Health Organizations

Depending on your specific arthritis-related problem, you may find helpful information from such organizations as the British Sjögren's Syndrome Association, Lupus UK or the National Osteoporosis Society. To find out whether there is a branch near you, contact the headquarters of the organization either by phone or on their web site, or try looking in your phone book. Your local library might also have a list of voluntary and self-help organizations in your area.

Central and Local Government

The Department of Health produces many publications on various matters relating to health. Similarly, the NHS publishes *A Guide to the NHS*, which outlines what services are available. And your local Primary Care Trust might well produce leaflets and booklets about services in your area, from time to time.

The NHS telephone helpline NHS Direct is also available online (see the section on the Internet, below).

The Internet

The Internet is a network of computers throughout the world that can exchange information almost instantaneously. The World Wide web is a system of electronic documents linked together and available on the Internet to anyone with a computer, a modem and an Internet service provider, such as America Online (AOL), CompuServe or Freeserve. Many libraries have Internet access.

If you have access to the Internet, you can find just about any type of information you could want. Some of the sources of information you can find on the Internet include:

- **Arthritis Care.** Arthritis Care's web site is packed with helpful information about arthritis and about the organization's publications, services, events and campaigns, and how you can get involved. There is also information and a helpline service for young people with arthritis. A list of other organizations, such as Carers UK and Lupus UK, will let you click onto those you are interested in and take you to their web sites as well.

- **The Arthritis Foundation**. The Foundation's web site (www.arthritis.org) has many helpful services, including a database of arthritis information that can be searched by key words and articles from current and past issues of its magazine *Arthritis Today*.

- **NHS Direct Online**. The web site includes a health encyclopaedia covering more than 400 topics, including different illnesses and conditions, tests, treatments (and a separate 'best treatments' section) and operations. It is also possible to complete and submit an online form setting out a particular query, if you cannot find the information you need on the web site. This will be researched by a health-information professional and you should receive a response within five working days.

- **Other voluntary health organizations.** There are other self-help organizations that exist to advise and support people with specific forms of arthritis. For example, the Children's Chronic Arthritis Association and the National Ankylosing Spondylitis Society.

- **Doctor's organizations.** Every group of medical specialists has a professional society, such as the British Society for Rheumatology (www.rheumatology.org.uk), the Royal College of General Practitioners (www.rcgp.org.uk), the Royal College of Physicians (www.rcplondon.ac.uk) and the Royal Colleges of Surgeons of Edinburgh and of London (www.rcsed.ac.uk; www.rcseng.ac.uk). Such web sites may include health information targeted to consumers and links to the organizations' medical journals.

- **Medical journals.** The contents of many medical journals (including those of past issues) can be found on the Internet. While the majority of journals offer full articles only to paid subscribers, many provide abstracts of articles free of charge to anyone who visits their web sites. Some sites allow you to purchase the full text of a single study. To locate journals specific to arthritis and related diseases, visit www.mednets.com/rheumatojournals.htm.

- **The National Institute of Arthritis and Musculoskeletal and Skin Diseases (NIAMS).** A branch of the US National Institutes of Health, NIAMS offers a variety of publications and other reliable, medically reviewed information on arthritis and related diseases that can be downloaded free of charge. You'll find information about NIAMS at www.nih.gov/niams.

- **The National Library of Medicine.** Operated by the US government, the library allows you to search its MEDLINE database – one of the largest, best known databases of medical information – free of charge. Once you have located a reference to an article of interest, you can order copies for a fee. Visit the library's web site at www.nlm.nih.gov.

- **Universities, pharmaceutical companies and hospitals.** There are countless other sources of arthritis information on the Internet, from university medical schools to commercial web sites designed to sell products. If you enter the word arthritis in any Internet search engine, you're likely to find thousands of matches. A few examples of good search engines are www.google.com, www.yahoo.com, www.excite.com and www.lycos.com.

- **Message boards and on-line support groups.** Message boards and on-line support groups let you 'talk' and share your thoughts, feelings, questions and suggestions with people from around the world. The US Arthritis Foundation's web site contains active message boards that let you chat with other people who have arthritis or related diseases. To read and post messages on the Arthritis Foundation's message board visit the Foundation's web site (www.arthritis.org) and click on Message Boards in the navigational bar. Arthritis Care does not yet have a message board but hopes to add this when the web site is redeveloped.

In these sources, you will find virtually limitless information that covers a variety of topics. Not everything will be relevant in the UK but it might still be of interest.

A word of warning. Remember that anyone can put up a web site containing any information that they wish to include. Some of it will be useless and some possibly downright dangerous. So look first at reputable web sites and see where they take you.

Other Information

As well as getting medical help, you may qualify for help from your local authority or the Department for Work and Pensions. Criteria vary from region to region so the information below is very general. If you think that you qualify for some sort of assistance, get in touch with your local authority's social services department.

Disability Living Allowance. Disability Living Allowance (DLA) is paid to people who have had care or mobility needs since they were less than 65 years of age. It is intended to help with the extra costs of disability, and is not means-tested. It has two components – the care component and the mobility component. The care component has three rates:

- lowest rate: for someone who needs help during the day
- middle rate: for someone who needs help during the day or the night
- highest rate: for someone who needs help both during the day and at night

The mobility component has two rates:

- lower rate: for someone who can walk but needs someone to guide or help them
- higher rate: for someone who cannot walk at all or is virtually unable to walk

The claim form for this allowance is lengthy and you can get help with filling it in from the Benefits Enquiry Line (contact details in the Resources section) or consult an experienced adviser at the Citizens Advice Bureau.

Attendance Allowance. Attendance Allowance (AA) is paid to people who have become disabled at the age of 65 or over. They may be entitled to this if they are severely disabled and have needed a great deal of care for at least six months. To qualify for this benefit they need frequent help, or continual supervision throughout the day to keep them safe. Needing help with eating or drinking, washing, showering or bathing, or getting about indoors would all qualify for this benefit.

Someone who repeatedly needs help at night would also qualify.

As with the Disability Living Allowance, the application form is quite long but don't be put off. An applicant might be asked to have a medical examination, which can be arranged in their own home if necessary.

Carer's Allowance. A 'carer' is anyone who looks after a relative, partner, spouse or even friend, of any age, who cannot manage without some help.

Anyone who cares for someone for at least 35 hours per week, with earnings of not more than £82 per week (2005 rate), may be eligible for Carer's Allowance. They do have to pay Income Tax on this allowance (depending, of course, on any other earnings). It is not means-tested so it does not depend on any savings

they may have. The person they are caring for has to be receiving Attendance Allowance (AA) or the higher rate of Disability Living Allowance (DLA).

Other state benefits. Other benefits that might be available to someone with disabling arthritis include Income Support, Jobseekers Allowance, Housing Benefit and Council Tax Benefit. For information about these and the other benefits outlined above, contact your local social services department or the local office of the Department for Work and Pensions, or the Benefits Enquiry Line.

Blue Badge. The Blue Badge (formerly Orange Badge) scheme is for people who have great difficulty walking but either can drive a car or are passengers in someone else's car. The Blue Badge allows their car to be parked in areas that otherwise restrict or prohibit parking. The rules vary from area to area, so it is worth checking them out. Application for a Blue Badge is made to the local authority.

PART TWO

TREATMENTS FOR ARTHRITIS

Taking Drugs For Arthritis

5

CHAPTER 5:
TAKING DRUGS FOR ARTHRITIS

Regardless of the type of arthritis you have or the kind of doctor you see, medications are likely to be part of your arthritis treatment plan. For that reason, it's as important to understand as much as you can about arthritis medications as it is to learn about the medical condition itself.

In Chapter 6, we'll discuss in some detail the various types of medication used to treat the different forms of arthritis and related diseases. However, as you begin to talk to your doctor about medication options or fill your first prescription for arthritis medication, you'll probably have more general questions, which we'll try to answer here.

GENERIC VS BRAND NAME

When your doctor writes a prescription, the items listed will probably be generic rather than brand names. A generic drug is one that is called by its chemical name, indicating what is in it; any pharmaceutical company can make and sell it. A brand name drug (also called a proprietary preparation) is identical to or very similar to a generic drug but is produced by a specific pharmaceutical company. A generic drug is almost always cheaper than a brand name drug. For instance, you will find that ibuprofen (generic) will be noticeably cheaper than, for example, Nurofen or Brufen (brand names)

and paracetamol will be cheaper than, say, Panadol.

Choosing generic rather than brand name is like choosing an own-store brand of frozen peas rather than a brand name counterpart. The packaging is different but the contents are the same.

Here's why costs differ. When a company develops a new drug, it applies for a patent, which prohibits anyone else from marketing the drug for 20 years. This time of exclusivity allows the company to recoup the costs of developing and testing the drug, which costs many millions per medication. After the patent has expired, other manufacturers may duplicate and market their own versions of the drug, called generics. Because makers of generic drugs don't have to repeat the extensive clinical trials to prove the safety and efficacy of their drugs, their expenses are much less and they can pass along those savings to you.

Although manufacturers of generic medications don't have to repeat the same rigorous tests that the manufacturer of the original drug must pass (see page 168 for clinical trials), they still must meet certain requirements. They must prove that their drug is chemically identical to the brand-name version (that is, its active ingredient is the same). However, the nonactive ingredients, such as dyes and fillers, may be different. So if you are allergic to certain dyes or fillers, such as lactose, that could be an important difference between generic and brand-name medications.

Unfortunately, these nonactive ingredients don't always appear on the labels of medications that you can get without a prescription, so the only way you can know how you will react to a generic is to try one. In the vast majority of cases, you'll probably never know the difference. In the rare event that you don't get the same relief as you do from the brand-name medication, or if you experience a reaction to a nonactive ingredient in a particular medication, your best bet is to try the same medication from another manufacturer. Ask your doctor or pharmacist for a recommendation.

The medications you get from the pharmacist will always be accompanied by instructions on how much to take and when. With prescribed drugs there should also be a 'patient information leaflet', which tells you about the drug and any possible side effects, and what to do if you experience an adverse effect.

PRESCRIPTION VS OVER THE COUNTER

You're scanning the shelves of your local pharmacy for something to ease your aching joints and you find literally dozens of medications labelled as a pain reliever, non-aspirin pain reliever, arthritis formula or nighttime pain reliever. What is the difference between all of these medications, and how do they differ from the medications a doctor prescribes?

Essentially, the difference between these drugs and prescription medications is that you don't need a prescription to get them. This is usually because they are not as strong as prescription-only medications but they are still serious medicine.

When it comes to arthritis medications, the two types you'll find over the counter are the analgesic medication paracetamol (*Panadol*) and four non-steroidal anti-inflammatory drugs (NSAIDs): ibuprofen (*Advil, Brufen, Nurofen*), naproxen sodium (*Synflex*), ketoprofen (*Orudis*) and aspirin (*Aspro, Disprin*). Although these drugs come in many formulations and in combination with other ingredients – such as caffeine to speed pain relief, antihistamines to cause drowsiness or a diuretic to ease bloating – these are the only over-the-counter medications you'll find to ease pain.

Gradually, a number of drugs that were once available only by prescription are becoming available over the counter.

The increasing availability of medications without a doctors' prescription has benefits and drawbacks. On the positive side, getting a medication has never been more convenient. You don't need an appointment with a doctor just to get a prescription for a medication or other type of treatment to ease the pain of a muscle strain or a mild ache in your joints.

On the negative side, people are more likely than ever to self-medicate, not realizing they have a condition that requires the care of a doctor. People also tend to think that anything they get over the counter is safe and that

Questions to Ask Your Doctor About Drugs

To get the greatest benefit – and least risk of adverse effects – from your medications, it's important to know as much as possible about what your doctor is prescribing. Here are some questions you might want to ask:

- What is the name of the medication?
- What type of drug is this medication?
- How is this medication expected to help me?
- Are there any special instructions for taking this drug?
- Are there side effects?
- What should I do if I experience side effects?
- How long should I expect to wait before noticing effects?
- What should I do if I miss a dose of this medication?
- Is it cheaper for me to buy it over the counter?
- Is there anything else I should know about this medication?

they can adjust the dosage as they see fit. This belief is not correct. Even if you are taking an over-the-counter medication, it's important to follow the directions exactly. You also should contact your doctor promptly if you suspect that you have had an adverse reaction or if symptoms don't improve.

It's important to understand that over-the-counter medications may be similar or identical to the ones prescribed by your doctor. Taking an over-the-counter medication along with your prescription may lead to an overdose. Tell your doctor about all the medications you are taking at any time, including over-the-counter treatments and herbal remedies.

TRADITIONAL VS 'ALTERNATIVE'

Before a medication can make it to market, it must first undergo a rigorous process to demonstrate its safety and effectiveness. Based on the results of numerous studies, the Medicines and Healthcare products Regulatory Agency (MHRA) gives its approval for the drug to be marketed.

'Alternative' medications, such as the nutritional supplements and herbal remedies you find in health-food stores and in your grocery store's natural remedies section, are not required to undergo that rigorous process, so there is no proof that the alternative remedy will be effective or safe. There also are no assurances that the package will contain what the label says. In fact, some recent studies showed that several products included potentially harmful ingredients that were not listed on the product labels. Many products did not contain the ingredients promised or they contained smaller amounts of ingredients than were listed on the labels.

If you're interested in trying an alternative medication, it's important that you talk to your doctor first. Some supplements may interact with over-the-counter or prescription medications, putting you at risk of dangerous side effects. For more information about alternative medication, see Chapter 12, 'Complementary Therapies for Arthritis'.

TAKING MEDICATIONS RESPONSIBLY

In most cases, your doctor will decide the medication you need and write the prescription for it, but you are the one who must get the prescription filled and take it at the intervals and in the way prescribed. You must report any problems with the medication to your doctor. Remember, you are the leader of your health-care team. When it comes to taking medications, you are in control. With that position of control comes responsibility.

Failure to take medications correctly can cause numerous problems, ranging from failure to obtain the medication's full benefits to experiencing dangerous medical problems. Any substance that is strong enough to help is strong enough to harm, particularly if you don't take it correctly. This goes for the medications your doctor prescribes as well as the medications and nutritional supplements you can buy without a prescription.

When talk turns to medication, you should tell your doctor if you are pregnant or allergic to any medications, drink alcohol, have health problems other than your arthritis, or take other prescription or over-the-counter medications.

To make the most of your medication and for safety's sake, you should ask your doctor the following questions about any medication he or she prescribes:

What is the name of the medication? It's important to know the medication's name and to make sure that what your pharmacist gives you has that same name. Because some medications have similar-looking names, mix-ups can occur.

Are there special instructions for taking the drug? Some drugs must be taken with food to minimize stomach distress, while others must be taken on an empty stomach to be absorbed properly. Some drugs must be taken at the same time every day, while other medications may be taken as needed.

How long will it be before I notice effects? If you're expecting to feel better by tomorrow, but the medication your doctor prescribed takes a month to produce any benefits, you need to know. On the other hand, if a medication is made to work quickly, there is no reason to continue taking it for months on end if you're not noticing any results.

What should I do if I miss a dose? No matter how conscientious you are about taking your medication, the time will probably come when you discover that you forgot to take a dose. What do you do? For most drugs, your doctor probably will recommend taking the missed dose as soon as you realize your error, and then resuming your regular schedule. If a lot of time has passed, however, it may be best to skip the missed dose and resume your medication with the next scheduled dose. If you're in doubt, it's always best to ask your doctor or pharmacist.

What should I do if I experience side effects? Although an adverse reaction may be sufficient reason to stop taking one drug immediately, abruptly stopping another one could be dangerous. Find out which side effects are likely to pass, which reactions may warrant a call to the doctor's surgery and which require immediate attention from a doctor or other health-care professional.

Is there anything else I should know about taking this medicine? Now is the time to address any other concerns you might have. For example, if you have trouble swallowing pills, make sure the medication you are taking

can be crushed and mixed with liquid. Some cannot; ask your pharmacist. If the drug your doctor prescribes is one of them, you'll need to ask for a medication that comes in a liquid solution.

If you still have questions about the medications your doctor prescribes, ask whether there are any pamphlets or leaflets that might help; Arthritis Care has a booklet on arthritis medications. Drug manufacturers' web sites or customer care help lines also offer information about their drugs. For general questions or concerns about medications, the sources listed in Chapter 4 may help.

In Chapter 6, we'll discuss some of the specific types of drugs your doctor might prescribe for your arthritis.

PAYING FOR YOUR MEDICATIONS

Unless you are one of the many people who can receive medicines free, you have to pay a fee for each item listed in a prescription. This can add up to quite a lot over the months, so there are two possibilities to consider. First, is to ask the pharmacist whether any of the items listed is cheaper to buy over the counter – ordinary painkillers, for example. The other possibility is to obtain a prepayment certificate (a 'season ticket'). If you need 15 or more items in a year, which (2005 prices) would cost you £97.50, you can buy a prepayment certificate for £99.20. (There is a shorter version, costing £33.90 for four months if you need more than 6 items in that period.)

Common Arthritis Drugs

6

CHAPTER 6:
COMMON ARTHRITIS DRUGS

As we discussed in Chapter 5, medications are likely to be a part of almost any arthritis treatment plan. The medications available today can, in many cases, ease pain, relieve inflammation, prevent dangerous disease complications, strengthen porous bone, lessen flares and slow, stop or even prevent joint damage.

In this chapter, we'll discuss some of the specific types of medications used in the treatment of arthritis and related conditions. The particular disease you have, as well as its symptoms and its severity, will dictate the type of medication your doctor prescribes. Some types of medications are used to treat a wide variety of diseases, while other treatments are unique for certain diseases.

Following are some of the medications that may be a part of your arthritis treatment plan.

NON-STEROIDAL ANTI-INFLAMMATORY DRUGS (NSAIDs)

No matter what form of arthritis you have, there's a pretty good chance that the first drug your doctor prescribes or recommends will be a non-steroidal anti-inflammatory drug (NSAID). The chances are that you have already taken such drugs on your own.

The class of drugs called NSAIDs includes one of the oldest and most widely used medications, aspirin, as well as the popular over-the-counter medications ibuprofen (*Advil*,

Brufen, Neurofen), ketoprofen (*Orudis*) and naproxen sodium (*Synflex*), which are available in higher doses on prescription. About a dozen other NSAIDs are available only on prescription.

All NSAIDs ease pain and inflammation by blocking the production of bodily chemicals called prostaglandins, which also play a role in numerous other bodily functions, including blood clotting, menstrual cramps, labour contractions and kidney function. The specific NSAID your doctor prescribes will depend on a number of factors, including the following:

Your doctor's familiarity with the drugs. Because there are so many different NSAIDs, most doctors select four or five that can be used for all patients.

What works best for you. For unknown reasons, some people seem to do better on certain NSAIDs than others. If your first – or second or third – NSAID doesn't significantly improve pain and inflammation, your doctor may try another.

Convenience. Some NSAIDs come in once-a-day formulations. If you prefer the convenience of taking just one pill a day, ask your doctor to prescribe that type. Be aware, however, that once-a-day medications are not the best option for all people. Because they stay in the body longer than drugs designed to be taken more frequently, they may not be safe for people whose bodies have trouble metabolizing the drugs or for those who are at increased risk of side effects.

Economics. Let's face it, some NSAIDs (particularly the ones that are available as generics) cost less than others. When all other factors are equal or similar, it makes sense to use the drug that will be least expensive to you or to the NHS.

Ulcer risk. One of the biggest factors in determining which NSAID your doctor will prescribe is whether you have had ulcers or are at increased risk of getting them. Taking NSAIDs, particularly for a long period and at high doses, can lead to gastric distress and bleeding. This effect is caused by the reduced levels of prostaglandins, the pain- and inflammation-causing chemicals that NSAIDs inhibit. Prostaglandins have other functions in the body, including protecting the stomach lining from its own gastric juices. When prostaglandins are hindered, so is that protection. If ulcers are a problem or a potential problem for you, your doctor may prescribe one of the following drugs:

- **COX-2 inhibitors.** One of the newest additions to arthritis treatment, these are a class of NSAIDs that reduce pain and inflammation without increasing the stomach's vulnerability to damage. Celecoxib (*Celebrex*) works by selectively inhibiting cyclooxygenase-2 (COX-2), the enzyme responsible for production of inflammatory prostaglandins involved in arthritis, without interfering with COX-1, a similar enzyme that is responsible for the production of prostaglandins that protect the stomach. Because significant problems were being experienced with the COX-2 inhibitor *Vioxx* (rofecoxib), it has been withdrawn from use. Celecoxib is still available but might also be withdrawn from general use.

- **Diclofenac and misoprostol.** Marketed under the name *Arthrotec*, this formulation combines the NSAID diclofenac with a synthetic prostaglandin to replace the stomach-protecting prostaglandins that the NSAID inhibits.

- **Other NSAIDs.** Other types of NSAIDs that might be easier on the stomach include buffered tablets, enteric-coated tablets that don't dissolve until they reach the small intestine, and time-released capsules or tablets that release the drug slowly into the bloodstream. Meloxicam is an NSAID with effects similar to COX-2 inhibitors and is therefore safer than celecoxib.

ANALGESICS

If your arthritis causes pain, you may benefit from an analgesic, or pain-relieving, medication. Analgesic medications are prescribed purely for pain relief – that is, they don't work against inflammation the way NSAIDs do.

The most commonly used and readily available analgesic is paracetamol (*Panadol*). Based

WHEN NSAIDs CAUSE STOMACH DISTRESS

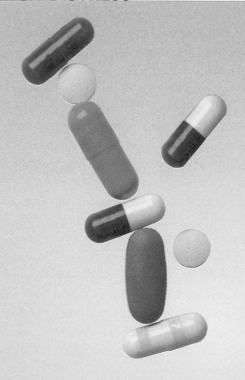

Any time you take a medication, you open yourself to the risk of side effects. If you're among the many people who take non-steroidal anti-inflammatory drugs (NSAIDs), the drugs prescribed most commonly for arthritis inflammation and pain and fever from other causes, the most likely side effects will involve your stomach.

Because traditional NSAIDs inhibit the body's production of prostaglandins, hormone-like substances that protect the stomach lining, using these drugs can lead to problems ranging from occasional nausea and heartburn to bleeding ulcers.

Fortunately, there are ways to minimize these risks. One method is using COX-2 inhibitors – NSAIDs designed to ease pain and inflammation without interfering with stomach protection. However, one (*Vioxx*) has been withdrawn from general use and the other (celecoxib) might follow.

Replacing prostaglandins. There is now a synthetic prostaglandin called misoprostol (*Cytotec*). By replacing the stomach's natural protective prostaglandins, misoprostol can reduce the risk of new ulcers or promote the healing of existing ulcers. One product, approved in recent years, combines the NSAID diclofenac sodium with misoprostol. Marketed under the name *Arthrotec*, the drug is available only on prescription.

Blocking stomach acid. Because neither COX-2s nor misoprostol reduce the risk of other gastrointestinal side effects (in fact, misoprostol is associated with increased abdominal pain and diarrhoea), if you have a problem with NSAID-related indigestion, heartburn or nausea, you may benefit from taking another medication with your NSAID.

Drugs that might be helpful come from two categories – histamine blockers (or H$_2$ blockers) and proton pump inhibitors – along with traditional NSAIDs. Both types of drugs work by reducing the amount of acid produced in the stomach. Histamine blockers include such drugs as cimetidine (*Tagamet*), ranitidine hydrochloride (*Zantac*), famotidine (*Pepcid*) and nizatidine (*Axid*). Proton pump inhibitors include omeprazole (*Losec*) and lansoprazole (*Zoton*). Neither proton pump inhibitors nor H$_2$ blockers decrease the risk of gastrointestinal bleeding.

Although some of these drugs (e.g. cimetidine, omeprazole and ranitidine) have become available over the counter, you should always check with your doctor before taking one of them with NSAIDs. One study suggested that H$_2$ blockers may mask the early symptoms of stomach ulcers.

Although NSAIDs can cause stomach problems – just as most medications might have side effects – they are very useful in controlling the pain of arthritis.

The Arthritis Care booklet *The Balanced Approach* is a useful guide to drugs and complementary therapies. Contact them (address on page 175) if you would like a copy, or download it from their web site.

on its cost, effectiveness and safety, paracetamol is generally recommended or prescribed as a first line of treatment against osteoarthritis pain. For many people, paracetamol alone is sufficient to ease the pain of osteoarthritis.

Paracetamol can be purchased over the counter under a variety of different trade and store names and often is the active ingredient in products labelled 'aspirin-free pain reliever'.

Until recently, paracetamol was the only analgesic used for day-to-day arthritis pain. Although doctors sometimes prescribed opiate analgesics such as oxycodone (*OxyNorm*) or dextropropoxyphene hydrochloride (*Doloxene*) for arthritis patients, these types of pain relievers traditionally have been used only for the acute pain of surgery or osteoporotic fracture or for severe musculoskeletal pain.

In recent years, however, the medical profession has begun to focus on the importance of treating nonmalignant pain and the unique ability of opiates to ease pain. (When the American College of Rheumatology revised its guidelines for treating osteoarthritis in 2000, it acknowledged, for the first time, the role of opiate analgesics in treating osteoarthritis pain. One analgesic, tramadol (*Zamadol, Zydol*), was mentioned specifically in the group's treatment guidelines.) Opiate drugs may carry the risk of dependence, causing some debate on their use for treating the pain associated with a chronic illness (see 'When NSAIDs Cause Stomach Distress' on page 62).

Because analgesic medications don't influence prostaglandin production the way NSAIDs do, they don't carry NSAIDs' risk of ulcers. They do, however, have side effects of their own, which may include drowsiness, grogginess and the potential for dependence.

TOPICAL OINTMENTS

If you find you can't take oral analgesics or if you have just a few joints or sore muscles that need soothing, you might want to try one of the many analgesic ointments, creams and gels available over the counter. There is a role for topical analgesics for the pain of osteo-arthritis, particularly in people whose pain is mild to moderate and not relieved by parac-etamol alone.

Unlike most other arthritis medications, which are swallowed or injected, these prep-arations work on the area on which you rub them, minimizing the risk of systemic side effects.

The effects of topical analgesics come from one or more active ingredients. Here are some of the most common ones:

Capsaicin. A highly purified natural ingredi-ent found in cayenne peppers, capsaicin works by depleting the amount of a neuro-transmitter called substance P that is believed to send pain messages to the brain. For the first couple of weeks of use, the ingredient may cause burning or stinging. Capsaicin is available under the product names *Axsain* and *Zacin*. *NatraFlex* includes both capsaicin and counterirritants.

Counterirritants. Like hitting your toe to take your mind off a headache, counterirritants

stimulate or irritate the nerve endings to distract the brain's attention from musculo-skeletal pain. Counterirritants include such substances as menthol, oil of wintergreen, camphor, eucalyptus oil, turpentine oil, dihydrochloride and methyl nicotinate and are found in such products as *Deep Relief* and *Tiger Balm*.

Salicylates. Like the salicylates found in many pain relievers you take as tablets, these compounds may work by inhibiting prostaglandins. In topical preparations, they act as counterirritants, stimulating or irritating nerve endings. Brand-name exam-ples of topical analgesics containing salicylates include *Deep Heat Rub*, *Movelat Gel* and *Ralgex*.

NSAIDs. Ointments can give relief in joints and muscles but without causing side effects. Brand names include *Fenbid*, *Ibugel*, *Ibuleve* and others.

CORTICOSTEROIDS

If you have an inflammatory disease, such as rheumatoid arthritis, lupus, polymyalgia rheumatica, polymyositis or an arthritis-related condition called giant cell arteritis, there's a good chance that your doctor will prescribe a corticosteroid medication for you. Corticosteroids (also called just 'steroids') are potent fighters of inflammation. They can help reduce harmful joint inflammation and control destructive inflammation of the kidneys, blood vessels and other organs.

The Opiates Debate

Some doctors would never prescribe opiates for arthritis or a related chronic disease. Others argue that they can be an appropriate drug for pain relief and promoting sleep. Even doctors who support their use agree that opiates are only necessary for a small number of people, and then only as part of a comprehensive treatment programme.

If pain relief is not achieved with NSAIDs, tricyclics, paracetamol or tramadol, then opiates such as codeine, hydrocodone, oxycodone or methadone may be considered. Before deciding to take this route, it is important for the patient to have full information about dependency and expected side effects. Some doctors might then ask the patient to sign a 'contract' outlining the appropriate use of the drugs and possible unwanted effects, to confirm that they both understand what is involved. Below are what many doctors view as central issues in the debate:

Advantages:

- Opiates are the most effective available medications for managing pain.
- The majority of arthritis patients don't need opiates. But those who do should have the option for a trial period.
- The addiction rate from opiates in this context is one per cent. Addiction (compulsive, self-destructive use) is not the same as dependence (withdrawal symptoms if the drug is stopped abruptly).
- Less pain results in better functioning.

Disadvantages:

- When you use opiates, you are treating pain solely as a symptom, without necessarily eliminating the factors that cause it. Therefore, opiates should be used only in the context of a thorough medical management programme.
- Dependence is an expected result of treatment.
- Opiates will dull pain, but not eliminate it. In other words, they are not a 'cure' for the pain associated with arthritis or related conditions.
- Tolerance to opiates occurs after a time – from months to years – so that increasing the dosage is necessary to maintain the same level of response.
- Opiates have side effects such as mental fuzziness, constipation and nausea.

The most-prescribed corticosteroid for arthritis-related diseases is prednisolone (*Deltacortril, Precortisyl* etc.), but there are several others, including cortisone and methylprednisolone.

Corticosteroids may be taken systemically, in pill form or by injection into a vein or muscle. If you have just one or a few inflamed joints, however, your doctor may inject a corticosteroid compound directly into the joints for quick, temporary relief without wide-ranging side effects. Corticosteroid creams are also available to treat arthritis-related rashes or psoriasis lesions.

When used in high doses or long-term, corticosteroids are associated with a number of side effects, including Cushing's syndrome (weight gain, 'moon' face, thin skin, muscle weakness, brittle bones), cataracts, hypertension, increased appetite, raised blood sugar, indigestion, insomnia, mood changes, nervousness and restlessness. Those risks can be minimized by using the lowest doses that control your disease.

Some doctors reduce the risk of corticosteroid side effects by prescribing alternate-day therapy (that is, you take your dose every other day, instead of every day).

DISEASE-MODIFYING ANTI-RHEUMATIC DRUGS (DMARDs)

Disease-modifying antirheumatic drugs (DMARDs) are a class of medications that doctors prescribe for rheumatoid arthritis and other inflammatory forms of arthritis, such as psoriatic arthritis or ankylosing spondylitis. As the name suggests, DMARDs actually modify the course of disease, slowing or even stopping its progression. Most of these drugs work by suppressing the immune system, which is involved in the joint damage that occurs in RA and other diseases.

If your doctor prescribes a disease-modifying antirheumatic drug, don't expect quick results. These drugs often take several weeks or months to produce effects, although most people find the results well worth the wait.

Not long ago, if you had seen a doctor about rheumatoid arthritis, you probably wouldn't have been prescribed a DMARD – at least not until all other drug options had been exhausted. That approach began to change a decade or so ago, as studies showed that irreparable joint damage often occurs early in the course of disease and that by prescribing DMARDs early on, doctors may be able to get the disease under control before such damage occurs. Doctors also are prescribing more combinations of DMARDs and finding that, for many patients, drug combinations provide benefits that a single drug can't offer.

In 1998, a drug called leflunomide (*Arava*) became one of just a few DMARDs developed specifically for rheumatoid arthritis.

Most DMARDs originally were used and approved for other medical conditions. Methotrexate, for example, originally was a cancer treatment. Ciclosporin (*Neoral, Sandimmun*) was used to prevent organ rejection in people who had undergone transplants, and hydroxychloroquine sulfate (*Plaquenil*) was used to treat malaria. It was only after years of use for these other conditions that these DMARDs were approved for the treatment of rheumatic diseases.

Despite the drugs developed in recent years, existing DMARDs continue to play an important role in managing rheumatoid arthritis. Methotrexate (*Maxtrex*), for example, is considered by many rheumatologists to be the 'gold standard' for RA treatment. Other DMARDs, including oral or injectable gold, are used much less frequently than they once were.

BIOLOGICAL RESPONSE MODIFIERS

Unlike traditional DMARDs, which may cause widespread suppression of the immune system, biological response modifiers (BRMs, or biological agents) target specific immune system components, such as chemical messengers called cytokines, that play a role in the inflammation and damage of the disease.

The three currently available agents, etanercept (*Enbrel*), infliximab (*Remicade*) and adalimumab (*Humira*), use different chemical actions to block an inflammatory cytokine called tumour necrosis factor (TNF), which is believed to play a role in RA and some other diseases. As a result, these agents retard the inflammatory response and ease the signs and symptoms of RA. However, ongoing research has shown that their effects go beyond symptomatic relief; both inhibit the progression of structural damage in patients with moderate to severely active rheumatoid arthritis. While some doctors reserve biological agents for patients whose arthritis hasn't responded well to more conventional therapies, others are starting to prescribe them earlier in the disease process in an effort to ward off or reduce permanent joint damage.

A disadvantage of these agents is that they must be injected. Etanercept is injected twice a week through a small needle just beneath the skin. Infliximab is administered intravenously every eight weeks in a two-hour out-patient procedure. Adalimumab injections are self-administered fortnightly. Another drawback is their cost – they are expensive.

Other biological agents in testing and development target other chemicals. One of the most promising newcomers to be approved is anakinra (*Kineret*), an agent that inhibits the action of an inflammatory cytokine called interleukin-1 (IL-1).

Some biological agents in development target more than one chemical. Some are being designed so that they can be taken orally.

MEDICATIONS FOR OSTEOPOROSIS

Just a decade ago, women had only two options when it came to preventing osteoporosis: take oestrogen replacement therapy or take their chances. For men at risk of this bone disease, oestrogen wasn't an option.

Today, however, there are an increasing number of options for women who have or are at risk of developing osteoporotic fractures. Recent additions to the drugs used are alendronate (*Fosamax*) and risedronate sodium (*Actonel*).

Medications for osteoporosis prevention or treatment fall into the following general categories. Whichever treatment your doctor prescribes, ask about the advisability of taking calcium and vitamin D supplements. See 'Nutrition for Healthy Bones' on page 71 for more information on calcium and vitamin D.

Hormones

Oestrogen. The most widely used osteoporosis medication for post-menopausal women is the female hormone oestrogen (e.g. *Premarin*). Before the menopause, high levels of oestrogen in the body help keep bone strong by causing the death of cells that are responsible for bone degradation. For women who have not had a hysterectomy, doctors prescribe oestrogen in combination with the hormone progesterone (e.g. *Premique*, *Prempak-C*) to minimize any risks of oestrogen on the uterus. If you are going through the menopause and experiencing troublesome hot flushes and other symptoms, oestrogen replacement can ease those symptoms as well as bone loss.

Calcitonin. Another hormone used to treat osteoporosis is calcitonin, which is similar to a hormone produced by our parathyroid glands (two pairs of endocrine glands that are situated behind or within the thyroid gland). Parathyroid hormone occurs naturally in the body, controls the distribution of calcium and phosphate, and has been shown to have an effect on bone growth. Calcitonin, which is administered by injection (*Forcaltonin*) or nasal spray (*Miacalcic*), has been shown to reduce fracture risk. It also has some pain-relieving effects for people who already have had fractures.

Bisphosphonates

A class of medication used in the treatment of bone diseases, including the arthritis-related condition Paget's disease, bisphosphonates are used increasingly in the treatment of osteoporosis because they inhibit bone resorption. In recent years, two bisphosphonate medications, alendronate (*Fosamax*) and risedronate sodium (*Actonel*), were approved for osteoporosis. Unlike many of the other medications used for osteoporosis, bisphosphonates are appropriate for men.

Selective Oestrogen Receptor Molecules

One of the newest classes of medications for osteoporosis, selective oestrogen (estrogen) receptor molecules (SERMs), including raloxifene hydrochloride (*Evista*), work much like oestrogen to slow bone loss. The biggest difference is that they lack some of oestrogen's side effects, mainly those related to breast and uterine tissue, making them an attractive alternative to oestrogen replacement for women at increased risk of breast or uterine cancer.

MEDICATIONS FOR FIBROMYALGIA

Although there aren't any drugs approved specifically for fibromyalgia, if you have the condition, you may benefit from some of the drugs used for arthritis pain – namely, NSAIDs or analgesics. Your doctor may also prescribe some medications that aren't commonly used in other forms of arthritis or related conditions.

Because studies have shown that lack of deep, restorative sleep is a common problem in people with fibromyalgia and that poor sleep quality contributes to the condition's characteristic muscle pain, fatigue and concentration difficulties, some of the most popular medications are those that promote deep sleep. These drugs include:

Antidepressants. When administered in smaller doses than those used to treat depression, antidepressant medications, including tricyclics – amitriptyline hydrochloride (*Elavil, Lentizol*), doxepin (*Sinequan*) and nortriptyline (*Allegron*) – and selective serotonin reuptake inhibitors (SSRIs) – fluoxetine (*Prozac*), paroxetine (*Seroxat*) and sertraline (*Lustral*) – may help people with fibromyalgia get the restorative sleep they need.

Although tricyclic antidepressants usually are the medications of choice for fibromyalgia-related sleep problems, research suggests that combining low doses of tricyclic antidepressants with SSRIs may increase each drug's benefits to people with fibromyalgia

Muscle relaxants. Muscle-relaxing medications, such as cyclobenzaprine, may help reduce muscle spasms associated with fibromyalgia and help induce deep sleep.

Anti-anxiety medications. Like antidepressants, anti-anxiety medications, such as temazepam (*Euhypnos*), may be given in low doses to promote sleep. Some doctors believe these drugs work by interfering with brainwave activity that keeps people with fibromyalgia in a superficial stage of sleep.

Other fibromyalgia treatments. Some of the newest sleep aids promise to be effective for people with fibromyalgia. These drugs include zolpidem (*Stilnoct*) and zaleplon (*Sonata*).

MEDICATIONS FOR GOUT

Whether you have had one gout attack or ten, chances are that you would do just about anything to keep from having another. Fortunately, there are medications that can ease or prevent future attacks. Determining which medication is right for you requires an understanding of the underlying problem.

Gout is caused when excess uric acid builds up in the body and is deposited as crystals in body tissues, including the joints and skin. If you have gout because your body produces too much uric acid, a drug called allopurinol (*Cosuric, Zyloric*) will slow the rate of uric acid production and help prevent future attacks. On the other hand, if the build-up is related to your body's inability to excrete uric acid properly, two other drugs – probenecid (*Benemid*) or sulfinpyrazone (*Anturan*) – may help prevent attacks by increasing the amount of uric acid passed in the urine.

Although preventing attacks is a goal for anyone with gout, medications used to prevent gout attacks do little, if anything, to ease an attack once it has started. Ironically, any of these drugs may, at first, cause an increase in gout attacks, as the body mobilizes uric acid. For that reason, your doctor should prescribe an NSAID or anti-inflammatory drug called colchicine along with these uric acid regulators to ease the pain and inflammation of attacks. Once an attack has started, NSAIDs or corticosteroids can provide symptomatic relief for gout.

WHERE TO LEARN MORE

To learn more about the drugs you take, you may want to check some of these other resources. Some are meant for doctors, but you may wish to know more about your drugs than is given in the accompanying 'patient information leaflets'.

Books

There are books that concentrate on drugs and their uses. Two that are written for the average person are:

- *Know Your Medicines* by Pat Blair, published by Age Concern England, answers questions commonly asked by patients about the medications they take: what they are for and how they work, dosages and safety.
- *Which? Medicines* by Rosalind Grant, published by the Consumers Association, discusses the various medications available for different diseases and conditions.

The *British National Formulary* (*BNF*) is published twice a year by the British Medical Association and the Royal Pharmaceutical Society of Great Britain. Listing medications used in the UK, it gives details of the chemical make-up of each drug, conditions or illnesses for which it is used, dosages, possible side effects and circumstances in which it should not be used or used only with caution. The book is aimed at pharmacists and doctors, so is not really intended for general readership.

Martindale's Complete Drug Reference is published every few years by the Pharmaceutical Press, London (the publishing arm of the Royal Pharmaceutical Society of Great Britain). It is a vast book that gives more detail than the *BNF*, including drugs used outside the UK. It, too, is intended for pharmacists rather than a general reader.

Web Sites

Pharmaceutical companies have their own web sites, which often have information for

NUTRITION FOR HEALTHY BONES

Whether you have osteoporosis or want to prevent it, it's essential that you get plenty of the bone-building mineral calcium. Calcium is available in dairy products, canned sardines or salmon with bones, fortified juices and green, leafy vegetables.

Vitamin D also is needed to help your body use the calcium you consume.

Dietary sources of vitamin D include fortified milk or dairy products, fortified breakfast cereals, egg yolks and oily fish.

Below are the Recommended Daily Allowances (RDAs) for calcium and vitamin D. As these lists show, requirements for the two nutrients vary with age. Consult your doctor or dietitian to learn more.

Daily Calcium Requirement

children 7–10 years	550 mg
girls 11–18 years	800 mg
boys 11–18 years	1,000 mg
all 19+ years	700 mg
men and women with osteoporosis	1,200 mg
PREGNANT OR BREASTFEEDING	
pregnant	700 mg
breastfeeding	1,200 mg

Daily Vitamin D Requirement

childhood, pregnancy, 65+	10 micrograms
adulthood	5 micrograms
70+ years	20 micrograms

If you live in a northern climate with limited exposure to full sun, or if you routinely wear sunscreen, your body may not make the amount of vitamin D it needs. Likewise, you may not be consuming enough vitamin D- and calcium-rich foods. If you think that you might not be getting enough of either nutrient, speak to your doctor or a dietitian about calcium and vitamin D supplements.

the general public. Sometimes they will have a separate web site for individual medications.

Other Sources of Information

Arthritis Care. The Arthritis Care booklet *The Balanced Approach* is a useful guide to drugs and complementary therapies. Contact them (address on page 175) if you would like a copy.

Patient information leaflets. Each prescription medication comes with a leaflet that details what it contains, how it should be taken, who should and who shouldn't take it, how it works, the possible side effects and what to do if you experience an adverse effect.

Your doctor and pharmacist. If you have any questions about a medication, how it works, or how to take it, the best thing to do is ask your doctor or your pharmacist. Ask your doctor any questions about side effects or how to take the medication when he or she is writing the prescription, or ask your pharmacist when you have the prescription filled.

Drugs Used in Treating Arthritis

NSAIDS: NON-STEROIDAL ANTI-INFLAMMATORY DRUGS

NOTE: Possible side effects for all NSAIDs, except where noted, include abdominal pain, dizziness, drowsiness, fluid retention, gastric ulcers and bleeding, greater susceptibility to bruising or bleeding from cuts, heartburn, indigestion, lightheadedness, nausea, nightmares, rash, ringing in the ears, reduction in kidney function, increase in liver enzymes.

Ulcers or internal bleeding can occur without warning. If you consume more than three alcoholic drinks per day, check with your doctor before using these products.

Aspirin
BRAND NAMES: *Anadin, Aspro, Disprin*
DOSAGE: 300 to 900 mg every 4 to 6 hours, maximum 4,000 mg daily

Choline salicylate
BRAND NAMES: *Audax, Dinnefords Teejel*
DOSAGE: 4,800 to 7,200 mg daily in several doses
OTHER POSSIBLE SIDE EFFECTS: Bloating, confusion, deafness, diarrhoea

Diclofenac potassium
BRAND NAME: *Voltarol Rapid*
DOSAGE: 75 to 150 mg per day in 2 or 3 doses

Diclofenac sodium
BRAND NAME: *Voltarol*
DOSAGE: 75 to 150 mg per day in 2 or 3 doses

Diclofenac sodium with misoprostol
BRAND NAME: *Arthrotec*
DOSAGE: 1 tablet 2 or 3 times per day

Diflunisal
BRAND NAME: *Dolobid*
DOSAGE: 500 to 1,500 mg per day in 2 or 3 doses

Etodolac
BRAND NAME: *Lodine*
DOSAGE: 600 mg per day in 1 or 2 doses

Drugs Used in Treating Arthritis

Fenoprofen calcium
BRAND NAME: *Fenopron*
DOSAGE: 900 to 2,400 mg per day in 3 or 4 doses; never more than 3,000 mg per day

Flurbiprofen
BRAND NAME: *Froben*
DOSAGE: 150 to 300 mg per day in 2 to 4 doses

Ibuprofen
BRAND NAMES: *Brufen, Nurofen*
DOSAGE: 1,200 to 2,400 mg per day in 3 or 4 doses for prescription-strength;
children over 7 kg weight 30 to 40 mg/kg per day in 3 or 4 doses

Indometacin
BRAND NAMES: *Artracin, Flexin, Indocin*
DOSAGE: 50 to 200 mg per day in 2 to 4 doses
OTHER POSSIBLE SIDE EFFECTS: Depression, headache, 'spacey' feeling

Ketoprofen
BRAND NAMES: *Orudis, Oruvail*
DOSAGE: 100 to 200 mg per day in 2 to 4 doses

Magnesium salicylate
BRAND NAME: *Doans*
DOSAGE: 2,600 to 4,800 mg per day in 3 to 6 doses
OTHER POSSIBLE SIDE EFFECTS: Bloating, confusion, deafness, diarrhoea

Meclofenamate sodium
BRAND NAME: *Meclomen*
DOSAGE: 200 to 400 mg per day in 4 doses

Mefenamic acid
BRAND NAME: *Ponstan*
DOSAGE: 500 mg 3 times a day

Meloxicam
BRAND NAME: *Mobic*
DOSAGE: 7.5 to 15 mg per day in 1 dose

Drugs Used in Treating Arthritis

Nabumetone
BRAND NAME: *Relifex*
DOSAGE: 1,000 mg at night

Naproxen
BRAND NAME: *Naprosyn*
DOSAGE: 500 to 1,000 mg per day in 2 doses

Naproxen sodium
BRAND NAME: *Synflex*
DOSAGE: 550 to 1,650 mg per day in 2 doses

Oxaprozin
BRAND NAME: *Daypro*
DOSAGE: 1,200 mg per day in 1 or 2 doses
or maximum 1,800 mg per day in 2 or 3 doses

Piroxicam
BRAND NAME: *Feldene*
DOSAGE: 20 mg per day in 2 or 3 doses, children over 6 years with juvenile arthritis
5 to 20 mg per day according to weight

Salsalate
BRAND NAME: *Disalcid*
DOSAGE: 1,000 to 3,000 mg per day in 2 or 3 doses
OTHER POSSIBLE SIDE EFFECTS: Bloating, confusion, deafness, diarrhoea

Sodium salicylate
BRAND NAME: *Doans Backache Pills*
DOSAGE: 3,600 to 5,400 mg per day in several doses
OTHER POSSIBLE SIDE EFFECTS: Bloating, confusion, deafness, diarrhoea

Sulindac
BRAND NAME: *Clinoril*
DOSAGE: 200 to 400 mg per day in 2 doses

Tolmetin sodium
BRAND NAME: *Tolectin*
DOSAGE: 1,200 to 1,800 mg per day in 3 doses

Drugs Used in Treating Arthritis

COX-2 INHIBITORS

Note: This class of NSAIDs blocks the prostaglandins involved in inflammation, but not the prostaglandins that protect the stomach lining. Therefore, COX-2 inhibitors may not have the stomach-related side effects of traditional NSAIDs. They are contraindicated, however, for people likely to be at risk of heart attacks and strokes.

Celecoxib
BRAND NAME: *Celebrex*
OA DOSAGE: 200 mg per day in 1 or 2 doses
RA DOSAGE: 200 to 400 mg per day in 2 doses
POSSIBLE SIDE EFFECTS: Same as other NSAIDs, except less likely to cause gastric ulcers and susceptibility to bruising and bleeding

ANALGESICS

These are drugs used for pain relief of arthritis and related conditions.

Dextropropoxyphene hydrochloride
BRAND NAME: *Doloxene*
DOSAGE: 65 mg every 4 hours as needed, no more than 390 mg per day
POSSIBLE SIDE EFFECTS: Dizziness or lightheadedness, drowsiness, nausea and vomiting

Paracetamol
BRAND NAME: *Panadol*
DOSAGE: 500 to 1,000 mg every 4 to 6 hours as needed, no more than 4,000 mg per day
POSSIBLE SIDE EFFECTS: When taken as prescribed, no side effects associated.

Paracetamol with codeine (co-codamol)
BRAND NAMES: *(a) Panadeine, Paracodol; (b) Codipart; (c) Kapake, Paradote, Solpadol, Tylex.* They come in several strengths: paracetamol 500 mg with codeine (a) 8 mg; (b) 15 mg; (c) 30 mg
DOSAGE: (a) 1 to 2 tablets every 4 to 6 hours, maximum 8 tablets daily; (b) and (c) 1 to 2 tablets every 4 hours, maximum 8 tablets daily
POSSIBLE SIDE EFFECTS: Constipation, dizziness or lightheadedness, drowsiness, nausea, unusual tiredness or weakness, vomiting

Drugs Used in Treating Arthritis

Paracetamol with dihydrocodeine (co-dydramol)
BRAND NAME: *Remedeine*
DOSAGE: 1 to 2 tablets every 4 to 6 hours as needed, maximum 8 tablets daily
POSSIBLE SIDE EFFECTS: Dizziness, drowsiness, lightheadedness, nausea or vomiting, unusual tiredness or weakness

Tramadol
BRAND NAMES: *Tramake, Zamadol, Zydol*
DOSAGE: 50 to 100 mg every 6 hours as needed
POSSIBLE SIDE EFFECTS: Dizziness, nausea, constipation, headache, sleepiness

TOPICAL ANALGESICS

Topical analgesics are ointments, creams and gels that are applied directly to the skin on the painful area. Topical analgesics should never be taken internally. If you are allergic to aspirin, do not use any topical analgesics containing salicylates, which contain the same medication as aspirin; and, of course, do not use any aspirin NSAID ointments. Never use any topical analgesic in conjunction with a heating pad, because deep burns could result. Read the labels for specific dosage information.

Capsaicin
BRAND NAMES: *Axsain, NatraFlex, Zacin*

Counterirritants
BRAND NAMES: *Feldene, Oruvail, Powergel, others*

Salicylates
BRAND NAMES: *Deep Heat, Dubam, Movelat, Transvasin, others*

NSAIDs (ibuprofen, ketoprofen, diclofenac, benzydamine, felbinac, piroxicam)
BRAND NAMES: *Fenbid, Ibugel, Ibuleve, Oruvail, others*

Drugs Used in Treating Arthritis

VISCOSUPPLEMENTS

In cases of knee osteoarthritis, viscosupplements may be injected directly into the joint to supplement hyaluronic acid, a substance that gives joint fluid its viscosity and that appears to break down in joints with osteoarthritis. These products relieve pain, but it is not known if they will work on other affected joints, or if they have benefits other than pain relief.

Avoid prolonged weight-bearing activities for 48 hours after injection. These products are not recommended for people allergic to bird feathers, bird proteins and/or eggs.

Possible side effects of both products include pain, fluid collection around the knee, swelling, heat and/or redness at the injection site.

Hyaluronate sodium
BRAND NAME: *Hyalgan, Supartz*

Hylan G-F 20
BRAND NAME: *Synvisc*

CORTICOSTEROIDS

Also known as steroids, these drugs are inflammation-fighting hormones. The following side effects are possible for all the following corticosteroids, but are more common with high doses and long-term use:

Cushing's syndrome (weight gain, 'moon' face, thin skin, muscle weakness, brittle bones), cataracts, hypertension, increased appetite, elevated blood sugar, indigestion, insomnia, mood changes, nervousness or restlessness. Dosage varies greatly based on disease severity.

Cortisone acetate
BRAND NAME: *Cortisyl*
DOSAGE: 25 to 30 mg per day

Dexamethasone
BRAND NAME: *Decadron*
DOSAGE: 0.5 to 10 mg per day in a single dose

Drugs Used in Treating Arthritis

Hydrocortisone
BRAND NAMES: *Hydrocortone* , *Solu-Cortef*
RA DOSAGE: 20 to 30 mg per day in a single dose or divided into several doses

Methylprednisolone
BRAND NAME: *Medrone*
DOSAGE: 2 to 40 mg per day in a single dose or divided into several doses

Prednisolone
BRAND NAME: *Deltacortril*
DOSAGE: 10 to 20 mg per day in a single dose initially, then 2.5 to 15 mg

Prednisone
BRAND NAMES: *Decortin, Meticorten, others*
DOSAGE: 1 to 60 mg per day in a single dose or divided into several doses

Triamcinolone
BRAND NAME: *Adcortyl*
DOSAGE: 4 to 48 mg per day in a single dose or divided into several doses

BIOLOGICAL RESPONSE MODIFIERS

NOTE: This new class of arthritis drugs blocks TNF (tumour necrosis factor), believed to play a major role in causing inflammation and joint damage. They may make patients more susceptible to infections. Little is known about their long-term side effects.

Adalimumab
BRAND NAME: *Humira*
DOSAGE: 40 mg once a fortnight, given by injection

Etanercept
BRAND NAME: *Enbrel*
DOSAGE: 25 mg twice per week, given by subcutaneous (beneath the skin) injection
POSSIBLE SIDE EFFECTS: Redness and/or itching, pain or swelling at the injection site

Infliximab
BRAND NAME: *Remicade*
DOSAGE: Determined by body weight. Drug is infused intravenously in a two-hour outpatient procedure every 1 to 2 months.
POSSIBLE SIDE EFFECTS: Upper respiratory infection, headache, nausea, coughing

Drugs Used in Treating Arthritis

NOTE: These drugs modify the course in inflammatory conditions. Minocycline, an antibiotic, is also included here. Many DMARDs are used in combination to increase effectiveness and decrease side effects. Explanations of cautions are contained in this chapter.

Auranofin (oral gold)

BRAND NAME: *Ridaura*

RA DOSAGE: 6 to 9 mg per day in 2 or 3 doses

POSSIBLE SIDE EFFECTS: Abdominal or stomach cramps or pain, bloated feeling, decrease in or loss of appetite, diarrhoea or loose stools, gas or indigestion, mouth sores, nausea or vomiting, skin rash or itching

Azathioprine

BRAND NAME: *Imuran*

DOSAGE: Based on body weight: 1 to 3 mg/kg daily

POSSIBLE SIDE EFFECTS: Cough, fever and chills, loss of appetite, nausea or vomiting, skin rash, unusual bleeding or bruising, unusual tiredness or weakness

Ciclosporin

BRAND NAMES: *Sandimmun, Neoral*

DOSAGE: Based on body weight: 2.5 to 5 mg/kg daily

POSSIBLE SIDE EFFECTS: Tender or enlarged gums, high blood pressure, increase in hair growth, kidney problems, loss of appetite, tremors

Cyclophosphamide

BRAND NAME: *Endoxana*

DOSAGE: From 2 to 15 mg/kg weight per week in a single dose; may also be given intravenously

POSSIBLE SIDE EFFECTS: Blood in urine or burning on urination, confusion or agitation, cough, dizziness, fever and chills, infertility in men and women, loss of appetite, missed menstrual periods, nausea or vomiting, unusual bleeding or bruising, unusual tiredness or weakness

Drugs Used in Treating Arthritis

Hydroxychloroquine sulfate
BRAND NAME: *Plaquenil*
DOSAGE: 200 to 400 mg per day in 1 or 2 doses
POSSIBLE SIDE EFFECTS: Black spots in visual field, diarrhoea, loss of appetite, nausea, rash

Leflunomide
BRAND NAME: *Arava*
DOSAGE: 10 to 20 mg per day in a single dose
POSSIBLE SIDE EFFECTS: Diarrhoea, skin rash, liver toxicity, hair loss

Methotrexate
BRAND NAME: *Maxtrex*
DOSAGE: 7.5 to 20 mg per week in 1 or 3 doses; may also be given by injection
POSSIBLE SIDE EFFECTS: Cough, diarrhoea, hair loss, loss of appetite, unusual bleeding or bruising, liver toxicity, lung toxicity

Minocycline
BRAND NAMES: *Minocin, Sebomin*
RA DOSAGE: 200 mg per day in 2 doses
POSSIBLE SIDE EFFECTS: Dizziness, vaginal infections, nausea, headache, skin rash

Penicillamine
BRAND NAMES: *Cuprimine, Depen*
RA DOSAGE: 200 mg per day in 2 doses
POSSIBLE SIDE EFFECTS: Diarrhoea, joint pain, lessening or loss of sense of taste, loss of appetite, fever, hives or itching, mouth sores, nausea or vomiting, skin rash, stomach pain, swollen glands, unusual bleeding or bruising, weakness

Sulfasalazine
BRAND NAME: *Salazopyrin*
RA DOSAGE: 500 mg 4 times per day
POSSIBLE SIDE EFFECTS: Stomach upset, diarrhoea, dizziness, headache, light sensitivity, itching, appetite loss, liver abnormalities, lowered blood count, nausea or vomiting, rash

Drugs Used in Treating Arthritis

Injectable gold (Sodium aurothiomalate and Aurothioglucose)
BRAND NAMES: Sodium aurothiomalate: *Myocrisin*; Aurothioglucose: *Aureotan*
DOSAGE: 10 mg in one dose the first week, 25 mg the following week, then 25 to 50 mg per week thereafter. Frequency may be reduced after several months.
POSSIBLE SIDE EFFECTS: Irritation or soreness of tongue, metallic taste, skin rash or itching, soreness, swelling or bleeding of gums, unusual bleeding or bruising

Oral gold
see Auranofin, page 80

FIBROMYALGIA DRUGS

At this time, there are no drugs specifically licensed for treating fibromyalgia. Here are some drugs that may alleviate certain symptoms associated with fibromyalgia, including pain, sleep problems and muscle aches.

Antidepressants
Antidepressants, including tricyclics and selective serotonin reuptake inhibitors (SSRIs), help people with fibromyalgia get the deep, restorative sleep they often lack.

TRICYCLICS

Amitriptyline hydrochloride
BRAND NAMES: *Domical, Elavil, Lentizol*
DOSAGE: 10 to 50 mg per day in a single dose
POSSIBLE SIDE EFFECTS: Difficulty concentrating, dizziness, drowsiness, dry mouth, headache, increased appetite (including craving for sweets), nausea, sleep disturbances, unpleasant taste, urinary retention, weakness or tiredness, weight gain

Drugs Used in Treating Arthritis

Doxepin

BRAND NAME: *Sinequan*

DOSAGE: 10 to 100 mg in the morning in a single dose

POSSIBLE SIDE EFFECTS: Difficulty concentrating, dizziness, drowsiness, dry mouth, headache, increased appetite (including craving for sweets), nausea, sleep disturbances, unpleasant taste, urinary retention, weakness or tiredness, weight gain

Nortriptyline

BRAND NAME: *Allegron*

DOSAGE: 10 to 100 mg in the morning in a single dose

POSSIBLE SIDE EFFECTS: Difficulty concentrating, dizziness, drowsiness, dry mouth, headache, increased appetite (including craving for sweets), nausea, sleep disturbances, unpleasant taste, urinary retention, weakness or tiredness, weight gain

SELECTIVE SEROTONIN REUPTAKE INHIBITORS (SSRIS)

Fluoxetine

BRAND NAME: *Prozac*

DOSAGE: 20 mg per day in a single dose

POSSIBLE SIDE EFFECTS: Anxiety and nervousness, diarrhoea, dry mouth, headache, increased sweating, nausea, trouble sleeping

Paroxetine

BRAND NAME: *Seroxat*

DOSAGE: 10 mg per day in a single dose

POSSIBLE SIDE EFFECTS: Constipation, decreased sexual ability, dizziness, dry mouth, headache, nausea, difficulty urinating, tremors, trouble sleeping, unusual tiredness or weakness, vomiting

Sertraline

BRAND NAME: *Lustral*

DOSAGE: 25 to 50 mg per day in a single dose

POSSIBLE SIDE EFFECTS: Decreased appetite or weight loss; decreased sexual drive or ability; diarrhoea; drowsiness; dryness of the mouth; headache, stomach or abdominal cramps, gas or pain; tremors; trouble sleeping; clumsiness or unsteadiness; dizziness or lightheadedness; slurred speech

Drugs Used in Treating Arthritis

BENZODIAZEPINES – SLEEP MEDICATION

Temazepam
BRAND NAMES: *Euhypnos, Normison*
DOSAGE: 10 to 20 mg per day in a single dose
POSSIBLE SIDE EFFECTS: When taken as prescribed, temazepam is not usually associated with side effects.

MUSCLE RELAXANTS

Cyclobenzaprine
BRAND NAMES: *Flexiban, Yurelax*
DOSAGE: 10 to 30 mg per day in 1 to 3 doses
POSSIBLE SIDE EFFECTS: Dizziness or lightheadedness, drowsiness, dry mouth, confusion

OTHER DRUGS USED FOR FIBROMYALGIA

Maprotiline
BRAND NAME: *Ludiomil*
DOSAGE: 25 to 150 mg per day in 1 to 3 doses
POSSIBLE SIDE EFFECTS: Blurred vision, decreased sexual ability, dizziness or lightheadedness, drowsiness, dry mouth, headache, increased or decreased sexual drive, tiredness or weakness

Trazodone
BRAND NAME: *Molipaxin*
DOSAGE: 50 to 150 mg per day in 2 or 3 doses
POSSIBLE SIDE EFFECTS: Dizziness or lightheadedness, drowsiness, dry mouth, headache, nausea and vomiting, unpleasant taste in mouth

Zolpidem
BRAND NAME: *Stilnoct*
DOSAGE: 10 mg per day in a single dose
POSSIBLE SIDE EFFECTS: Side effects are uncommon at prescribed dosage.

Drugs Used in Treating Arthritis

GOUT DRUGS

Allopurinol
BRAND NAMES: *Cosuric, Zyloric*
DOSAGE: 100 to 300 mg per day in a single dose
POSSIBLE SIDE EFFECTS: Hives, itching, liver-function abnormalities, nausea, skin rash or sores

Colchicine
BRAND NAME: Available only as generic
DOSAGE: 0.5 to 1.5 mg per day in 2 to 3 doses for prevention. 0.5 or 0.6 mg
every 2 or 3 hours (maximum 6 mg per day) to stop acute attacks.
POSSIBLE SIDE EFFECTS: Diarrhoea, nausea and vomiting, stomach pain

Probenecid
BRAND NAME: *Benemid*
DOSAGE: 500 to 1,000 mg per day in 2 doses
POSSIBLE SIDE EFFECTS: Headache, joint pain and swelling, loss of appetite, nausea, skin
rash, vomiting

Probenecid and colchicine (USA)
BRAND NAMES: *ColBenemid, Proben-C*
DOSAGE: 1 tablet (500 mg probenecid and 0.5 mg colchicine) 1 or 2 times per day
POSSIBLE SIDE EFFECTS: Diarrhoea, nausea and vomiting, stomach pain, headache, joint
pain and swelling, loss of appetite, skin rash

Sulfinpyrazone
BRAND NAME: *Anturan*
DOSAGE: 100 to 600 mg per day in 1 or 2 doses
POSSIBLE SIDE EFFECTS: Lowered blood count, rash, stomach pain

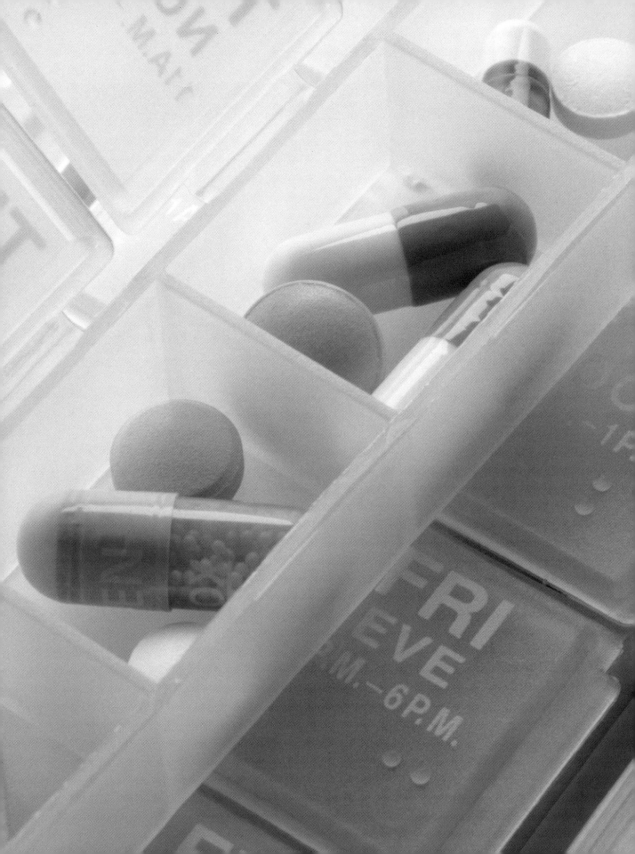

Combination Therapy and Other Options

7

CHAPTER 7:
COMBINATION THERAPY AND OTHER OPTIONS

WHEN ONE DRUG ISN'T ENOUGH

Despite the plethora of medications available for treating almost every form of arthritis, it's unlikely that one drug will relieve all of your symptoms or that drugs alone will be the answer to treating your arthritis. Here, we will discuss what you can do when one drug isn't enough, and in later chapters, you'll learn about a variety of non-medication options that are equally important in managing your disease.

With all the drugs available, and new ones continuously being developed, there is some treatment to help almost anyone with arthritis. However, it's the rare individual who will find a single drug that works for all signs and symptoms of the disease. For most people, treating arthritis effectively requires a combination of drugs and other treatments.

For example, if you have rheumatoid arthritis, you may take an NSAID to help ease pain and inflammation and take a DMARD, or a combination of DMARDs, to get your disease under control. If you have lupus, you may take a DMARD, such as hydroxychloroquine sulfate (*Plaquenil*), to help control the disease, and a corticosteroid medication to help prevent inflammation-related damage to internal organs such as the kidneys.

Not only will drugs most likely be used in combination with others, but the specific drugs and combinations can change over time, due to a number of factors, including the following situations.

When a Particular Drug No Longer Seems Effective

If you have been taking the same medication for your arthritis for a couple of years and notice that you're not doing as well as you were after your first months on the medication, it may be time to speak to your doctor about trying a different medication or adding another drug.

Some drugs are highly effective when they are first prescribed, but seem to lose their effectiveness over time. It is not clear whether the drugs actually become less effective over time or whether the disease becomes more active. Regardless, a change in medication may be in order.

When You Need More Than One Drug

Just as different types of medications work to ease different signs and symptoms of disease, different DMARDs may be necessary, in some cases, to get the disease under control. If your old medication doesn't seem to be working as well as it used to, or if a DMARD hasn't produced the expected effects after a few months of use, your doctor may add a medication to the regimen, rather than switch to a new medication. The DMARD combinations used most commonly for RA include methotrexate (*Maxtrex*), hydroxychloroquine (*Plaquenil*) and sulfasalazine (*Salazopyrin*); and methotrexate and ciclosporin (*Neoral, Sandimmun*). Although research has shown such combinations are effective for some people, there have been no studies comparing the different DMARD combinations to one another.

Increasingly, doctors have begun to prescribe one of the new biological agents with methotrexate for people with rheumatoid arthritis who do not achieve desired results with methotrexate alone. Some doctors also prescribe methotrexate with the new DMARD leflunomide (*Arava*).

Development of Other Medical Conditions

Some of the medications that help arthritis can actually worsen or cause unwanted effects in other diseases. For example, the development of hypertension might make it inadvisable to use corticosteroid medications, which can contribute to high blood pressure. Kidney or liver disease may necessitate discontinuing certain gout medications or many disease-modifying drugs, such as azathioprine, cyclophosphamide and leflunomide, which are metabolized by the liver and excreted through the kidneys. Stomach ulcers may mean that you can't take certain NSAIDs or the osteoporosis drug alendronate, which can increase

ulcer risk or worsen existing ulcers. Development of certain cancers or lupus-related blood clots, which oestrogen can exacerbate, may mean you can't take oestrogen replacement therapy for osteoporosis.

Even a natural condition like pregnancy can make a big difference in your medication regimen. While some arthritis medications are considered safe in pregnancy, several are off-limits, and the advisability of others depends on the particular stage of pregnancy.

Just as certain medical conditions may influence your doctor's prescribing decisions, so can the medications you take for those other conditions. In many cases, medications don't mix, so taking a certain medication for one condition may mean you have to forego a particular medication for another.

For example, if you have a clotting disorder that requires treatment with blood thinners, your doctor may advise against using aspirin and other NSAIDs that affect blood clotting. If you use antidepressant medications, your doctor may advise against your using opiate analgesics for pain, because of the drugs' cumulative effects on the central nervous system. If you take allopurinol for gout, you may not be able to take the DMARD azathioprine (*Imuran*).

If the drugs you need to take for different conditions can't be taken together safely, your doctor will need to determine which of the drugs is more important for your health and well-being, and which drug is less essential or can be more safely or effectively replaced with another medication.

Nutritional supplements can have dangerous effects when mixed with prescription or over-the-counter medications. Nutritional supplements are products such as herbs, minerals and enzymes that are purported to promote good health but are not regulated the way medications are. (For more on nutritional supplements, see Chapter 12, 'Complementary Therapies for Arthritis'.) Several supplements, including the memory enhancer ginkgo biloba and the migraine remedy feverfew, can add to the blood-thinning effects of certain NSAIDs, possibly increasing a patient's risk of gastrointestinal bleeding.

In all cases, it's best to discuss with your doctor any medical problems you have, and the medications and nutritional supplements you take for them. Some health problems may make a difference in the medication you are prescribed initially, and some may necessitate changes in your current medication.

NEW TREATMENT APPROACHES

In addition to changes in or additions to medications, there are some new treatment approaches your doctor may use when the drugs you are taking don't control your disease. Below are some possible new options.

Viscosupplements

If you have OA pain of the knee that hasn't been relieved by NSAIDs or analgesic medications, or if you can't or choose not to take medications, a couple of relatively new products – hyaluronate sodium (*Hyalgan, Supartz*) and hylan G-F 20 (*Synvisc*) – may help.

Often referred to as viscosupplements, these products are delivered directly into the knee through a course of three or five injections. Although the products' action is not well understood, they are believed to work by replacing hyaluronic acid, a substance that gives joint fluid its viscosity. Hyaluronic acid production seems to break down in joints with OA.

Both products relieve pain and are most effective for people with mild to moderate knee OA. So far, the products are not approved for injection into joints other than the knee, nor is it known whether they would provide the same pain-relieving effects for other joints.

Prosorba Column Therapy

One of the newest approaches to the treatment of rheumatoid arthritis in the USA – which has not reached the UK – involves not medication, but a cylinder about the size of a soup tin. The cylinder, called the *Prosorba* column, contains a sandlike substance, silica coated with protein A, which is a material that binds to antibodies associated with RA. The antibodies are then removed from the blood.

Protein A immunoadsorption therapy (*Prosorba* column therapy) is approved in the USA for people whose RA has not responded to disease- modifying antirheumatic drugs. The procedure typically takes place in a blood bank or a hospital's apheresis centre. It is administered in 12 weekly sessions, each lasting two to two-and-a-half hours.

Exactly how the procedure reduces joint

inflammation is unknown. Unwanted effects of treatment include a temporary, flu-like condition with chills, mild fever, nausea and fatigue. In rare cases, patients experience a rash that could make it necessary to discontinue treatment.

A TREATMENT FOR EVERYONE

By working closely with your doctor and being open about how well a treatment is working or not working, you are almost certain to find a treatment or combination of treatments that will ease your symptoms and, perhaps, control your disease. The shortcoming of all arthritis medications, as well as the newer treatment options, however, is that none can undo the damage that arthritis has already caused.

Fortunately, in many cases, surgery can help. Through modern surgical techniques, orthopaedic surgeons can repair soft-tissue injuries and damage, and they can replace damaged joints with durable (and painless) synthetic ones.

Although most people with arthritis will never require joint replacement surgery, surgery of some type is fairly common in the treatment of joint injuries or arthritis.

In Chapter 8, we'll discuss some of the surgical options available when medications and other non-medication options aren't enough to manage the disease.

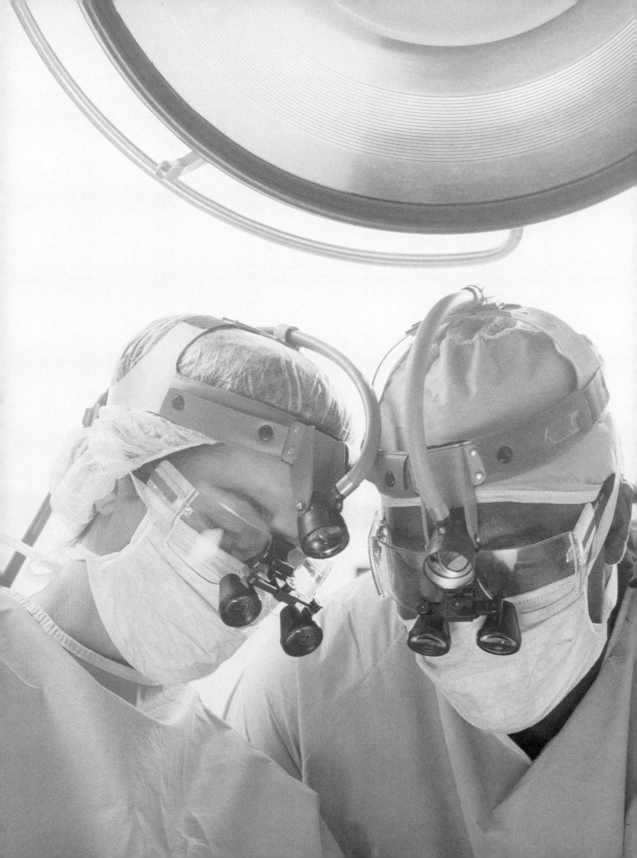

Surgery for Arthritis

8

CHAPTER 8: SURGERY FOR ARTHRITIS

For most people with arthritis, a combination of medications, exercise and joint protection techniques are sufficient for managing the disease. But when joint pain is severe and unrelenting, or when arthritis causes serious disability, surgery may be an effective option.

If you and your rheumatologist or GP believe that surgery is an appropriate option for you, your doctor will refer you to an orthopaedic surgeon, a doctor who specializes in surgery involving the musculoskeletal system. The surgeon can work with you to determine the type of surgery you need, how to prepare for surgery and what to expect before and after surgery. There are many different types of arthritis operations. The best type for you, if you need surgery, will depend on a number of factors, including the particular problem and its severity, the particular joint or joints involved, your age and your treatment goals.

DIFFERENT TYPES OF SURGERY

Surgery for arthritis is common, and the range of operations performed varies greatly – from simple outpatient procedures in which your joint damage is viewed through an arthroscope, to complete replacement of a damaged joint with a new prosthetic one.

Some operations may have you back to work within days, while others require months of activity limitations and physio-

therapy. What most of these operations have in common is that they offer the opportunity for less pain and improved function. Below are some of the most common types of surgery for arthritis.

Synovectomy

Synovectomy is the removal of the diseased synovium or the membrane that lines the joint. In diseases like RA, the synovium becomes inflamed, causing joint pain, swelling and disability. Removing the synovium can reduce symptoms and prevent or slow destruction of the affected joint.

In most cases, a technique called synovectomy is performed through arthroscopy (see page 96). In some cases, particularly if a large joint is involved, a surgeon may use a conventional incision.

Synovectomy isn't always permanent. In time, the diseased synovium often grows back, necessitating another synovectomy or, possibly, joint replacement surgery.

Osteotomy

Osteotomy is the correction of bone deformity by cutting and repositioning the bone, then resetting it in a better position. The most common arthritis-related use of osteotomy for arthritis is to correct curving of the tibia (shin bone) and improve the weight-bearing position of the lower leg in people with osteoarthritis of the knee. Osteotomy of the pelvis may be used to correct misalignment of the hip joint that leads to excessive cartilage wear and damage, but in general, the predictability of success in osteotomy is less than that of total joint replacement. For some people, however, the procedure offers pain relief. Recovery and new bone growth take several weeks.

Resection

Resection involves removing a portion of the bone from a stiff or immobile joint, which creates a space between the bone and the joint. Although the bone itself never grows back, more flexible scar tissue fills the space and offers more flexibility. However, the joint is less stable. Resection is most common in upper extremities, such as the wrist, thumb or elbow, and in the foot.

Arthrodesis

Arthrodesis, also called bone fusion, relieves pain, usually in joints of the ankles, wrists, fingers and thumbs. In arthrodesis, the cartilage is removed from the ends of the two bones forming a joint, and the bones are positioned together and immobilized, often with a pin or rod. After a while, the two bones join to form a single, rigid unit. Although the fused joint loses flexibility, it can bear weight better, is more stable and no longer causes pain. In other words, the joint will be painless and sturdy, but you will not be able to bend it.

Arthrodesis is often used for joints that aren't commonly replaced with prostheses. It is effective for people who, for reasons such as joint infections or poor bone quality, aren't good candidates for total joint replacement surgery.

Arthroplasty or Total Joint Replacement

Arthroplasty, or total joint replacement, refers to the procedure by which damaged joints are surgically removed and replaced with metal, ceramic and plastic parts. This common procedure has been used widely for many years, with excellent results.

The joints replaced most commonly and successfully are those of the hip and knee. Smaller joints, including the shoulders, elbows and knuckles, also can be replaced.

When joint replacement was first performed in the 1960s, the prosthetic components were always cemented in place. The cement often cracked or broke down, causing the joint to loosen over the course of several years. Surgeons began searching for a better way, and the search led to development of a new method called biological fixation; to keep prosthetic joints in place, the surfaces of the prostheses are porous, allowing the patient's own bone to grow into the prosthesis and hold it in place.

For younger people who have good bone growth into the prosthesis, some surgeons believe the result of an uncemented prosthesis may be a more durable, longer-lasting joint replacement. For older people, whose bone may not grow well enough to hold the prosthesis, cemented prostheses still are preferred. Sometimes, surgeons use a hybrid joint, in

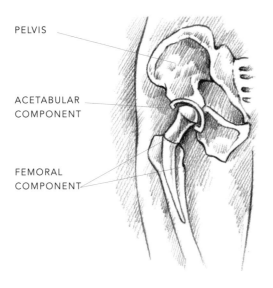

PELVIS

ACETABULAR
COMPONENT

FEMORAL
COMPONENT

HIP REPLACEMENT

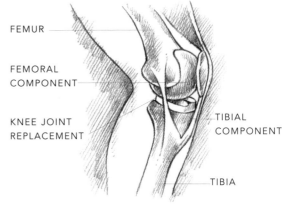

FEMUR

FEMORAL
COMPONENT

KNEE JOINT
REPLACEMENT

TIBIAL
COMPONENT

TIBIA

KNEE REPLACEMENT

which one component is cemented and the other is not. Fortunately, the development of better cements has improved the longevity of cemented joints. Because of this improvement, some surgeons prefer to use cemented joints.

Whatever type of prosthesis is used, you can expect your new joint to last 10 to 15 years or more. If a joint wears out or loosens, a second operation will be necessary to put in a new joint. Unfortunately, subsequent replacements tend to be less successful than initial ones, Nevertheless, quality of life is impoertant, so surgeons undertake joint replacement in younger patients rather than reserve it for those whose life expectancy is nearer that of prosthetic joints.

Arthroscopy

Arthroscopy is a process that allows a doctor to see directly into the joint through an arthroscope, a thin tube with a light at the end. An image of the joint's interior is transmitted to a closed-circuit television screen. The arthroscope is inserted through a small incision in the skin, and additional incisions may be used to insert small surgical tools.

Although you have probably heard about arthroscopy most often in connection with sports injuries in professional athletes, the procedure can be used for arthritis treatment and diagnostic purposes. Common uses for arthroscopy in treatment include removing a piece of loose tissue that is causing pain, repairing torn cartilage or smoothing a joint where the surface has become rough. More extensive surgery, such as synovectomy, or reconstruction of ligaments supporting a joint also can be done arthroscopically.

The advantage of arthroscopic surgery is that it requires less anaesthesia and less cutting than a standard operation. It is often done on an outpatient basis, eliminating the need for a hospital stay. Furthermore, patients recover from arthroscopy much more quickly than they do from some other types of surgery, and they can get back to normal activities more quickly.

Arthroscopy is used most often on the knee or shoulder, but increasingly, it is being used to treat damage found in other joints affected by injury or arthritis, such as the elbow, hip, wrist and ankle.

IS SURGERY THE RIGHT OPTION?

If arthritis is disabling and hasn't responded to medical therapies or such non-medication treatments as physiotherapy or exercise, or if you can't tolerate medications, surgery may be an appropriate option.

Your doctor and a surgeon will determine if surgery – and if so, what type of surgery – might help you. You will play a role in that decision, too, because in many cases, the decision to have surgery is a personal judgement call. Are you willing to undergo major surgery and weeks or months of rehabilitation for the prospect of having a pain-free joint and improved function, possibly for the rest of your life? Would you undergo the risks of surgery, such as potential infections, blood clots or anaesthesia complications, for the opportunity to be mobile and maintain your independence?

As you consider whether or not to have surgery, keep in mind that every person's situation is different. You may not benefit from the same surgery that a friend, family member or the majority of participants in a medical study did. Your doctor may advise against a particular operation or warn you that its chances of success are low. Even if your doctor thinks that surgery can help you, there are many factors that both you and your doctor must consider, including the following:

- **Other health problems.** If you have heart disease or lung disease, the strain of some types of surgery may be too much for you. Before having any kind of surgery, it's important to have other health problems under control.

- **Your medications.** In some cases, you may need to stop some of the medications you are taking for a while before surgery. For example, such drugs as aspirin and other non-steroidal anti-inflammatory drugs, which you may be taking to ease pain and inflammation, may interfere with blood clotting and cause you to bleed excessively during surgery. On the other hand, corticosteroid medications, such as prednisone, may be needed at larger doses during surgery. The reason is that these drugs are similar to hormones our bodies produce naturally in response to stress. In people who take synthetic corticosteroids, the body's ability to increase its own production of these hormones may be hampered. Therefore, additional medication may be necessary to help your body meet the demands of the situation.

- **Infections.** If you have any type of bacterial infection in your body, even an abscessed tooth, you'll need to have it cleared up before you undergo any surgery. One possible problem after joint surgery is infection, which can spread from another part of your body to your joint through the bloodstream.

- **Your weight.** If you are overweight, it's best to start losing weight before you decide to have surgery. Being overweight may put extra stress on your heart and lungs during surgery. If you are undergoing knee- or hip-replacement surgery, excess weight can be stressful on a prosthetic joint component. For any surgery involving a weight-bearing joint, excess body weight can make rehabilitation more difficult by placing strain on the joint and making it more difficult to do the exercises needed to make the joint stronger after surgery.

A loss of 10 per cent of your body weight can make a difference, but for many people, losing this amount of weight takes a well-designed diet and exercise programme as well as commitment and willpower. Consult your doctor if you're not sure if you need to lose weight or, if you do need to lose, how to best go about it.

- **Strength and fitness.** Although any rehabilitation programme after surgery will involve exercises to strengthen the muscles around the affected joint, doing such exercises beforehand may increase your odds of surgi-cal success. Similarly, aerobic exercise can prepare your heart and lungs for the rigors of surgery and rehabilitation. To learn more about what you can do to improve your physical fitness before surgery, consult your doctor or a physiotherapist.

- **Your care as you recuperate.** One of your major concerns as you consider surgery may be caring for yourself in the days and weeks that follow. Things to consider include: Who will care for your home, children, pets or plants while you are in the hospital? Who will care for you once you are home? Depending on the type of surgery you have, it may be a few days or a couple of months before you are able to do such things as stand for prolonged periods, drive a car, vacuum or shower without the assistance of another adult. Consider your personal support systems – or the possibility of getting someone to help you for a while – before the operation.

If you prepare properly for surgery, you'll have less to do or be concerned about when the time arrives, and relieving yourself of that stress now may help you recuperate faster. Nevertheless, recovering from surgery – particularly major surgery, such as total joint replacement or resection – requires a commitment. The amount of work you put into a recovery process often makes the difference between success and failure and your risk of adverse effects. In general, here's what you can expect to do following major joint surgery:

- **Wear support stockings.** Immediately after surgery and until you are up and moving, your doctor will want you to wear tight, elasticated stockings on your lower legs to prevent blood clots from forming in them. Blood clots, which can break loose and clog an artery, are among the most common and dangerous complications of joint replacement surgery.

- **Work your muscles.** Following surgery, and maybe even before, your doctor will probably refer you to a physiotherapist who will give you a programme of exercises that help strengthen the muscles that support the joint. It's important that you follow the programme faithfully, even when it may be painful to do so, to gain as much use of the joint as possible. Exercise will begin gradually and become progressively more strenuous as your joint gains strength and mobility.

- **Protect your joints.** Immediately after replacement surgery of the knee or hip, and for about six weeks after surgery, you'll need support when you walk. At first, you'll use a walker, and later, you'll graduate to a walking stick. You may need to wear a brace on the joint and use special, strategically placed pillows when you lie down.

Protecting a joint after surgery is important, regardless of the type of surgery you have. Your doctor, surgeon, nurse and physiotherapist will give you advice on joint protection.

- **Heed limits.** As you start to feel better, you may be tempted to do too much too soon. Resist this temptation. Using your joint more than it's ready to be used or moving the joint beyond its intended range of motion can cause damage and possibly necessitate further surgery. While prescribed exercise is essential, attempting to climb stairs, ride a horse or do jumping jacks shortly after joint replacement may cause your new joint to dislocate and can send you back to the hospital. If your new joint is one that relies on biological fixation ('cementless' joint replacement) to stay in place, you may have more severe activity restrictions as the new bone grows into the prosthesis to hold it in place. Because joint cement hardens quickly, there may be fewer initial restrictions on a joint that is cemented in place.

Be sure to do all the exercises your doctor and physiotherapist recommend, but also be sure to know and heed your joint's limits. If you have any doubt as to whether an activity is safe, consult your doctor.

- **Take your medications.** It's important that you take any medications your doctor prescribes exactly as directed. Medications you may need following surgery include opiate analgesics to relieve pain and make it easier to perform your exercises; blood thinners to reduce the risk of blood clots; antibiotics to reduce infection risk; and, of course, any medications you need for your arthritis control, including any NSAIDs, corticosteroids or DMARDs that you usually take. Although the joint on which you had surgery will soon feel better, unfortunately, the surgery will not slow damage or inflammation to other joints.

- **Steer clear of infection.** Even after you've recovered from surgery, it's important that you take extra precautions against bacterial infection if you have a joint prosthesis (or any type of implant in your body). For example, if you cut your finger on a kitchen knife or step on a nail, it's important that you do not let the wound become infected. There is the possibility that any infection that enters the body through the bloodstream may settle in the joint, causing problems that might require further surgery to correct. If you need to have any dental treatment done, let your dentist know that you have an artificial joint, so that extra precautions can be taken if necessary. In the past it was common practice to give a course of antibiotics to people in such circumstances but this has been discontinued because it is felt that the potential benefit is outweighed by the possibility of adverse effects.

By preparing for joint surgery and following doctors' orders and common sense afterwards, the operation may offer a lifetime of pain relief and increased mobility. As with any operation, however, joint surgery offers no guarantees. In rare instances, joint surgery results in infection, which requires further treatment or surgery. Prostheses have a limited life expectancy in even the best of circumstances, so if you have joint replacement as a young adult or in middle age, there's a chance that the prosthesis will loosen and have to be replaced in time.

Because surgery may be less successful the second, or third, time around, and most people don't want to face the prospect of another operation, age may be a major factor in your decision to have a joint replaced. Fortunately, there are many medications and other measures that can delay or eliminate the need for joint surgery. For those who do undergo joint replacement, advances in materials and surgical techniques are making the procedure work better and the joints last longer.

ANAESTHESIA: TO SLEEP OR NOT TO SLEEP

Regardless of the type of surgery you have, it's almost a certainty that you will need some type of anaesthesia. While most people associate anaesthesia only with pain relief, it has an additional purpose in the operating room – it allows the surgical team to control a wide range of natural bodily reflexes, such as heart rate and blood pressure, that could fluctuate dangerously in response to the trauma of surgery.

Your surgeon will recommend one of three types of anaesthesia – general, regional or local – to block your pain and control your natural bodily reflexes.

General Anaesthesia

General anaesthesia temporarily stops the brain's overall ability to sense and remember pain. Under general anaesthesia, which you breathe in through a face mask, you are asleep. When you awaken, you may have vivid memories of the hours and minutes leading up to surgery. You may even remember being wheeled into the operating room and being asked to count backwards as the anaesthetic put you to sleep. However, you will have no recollection of the time you were asleep or of the surgery itself.

Local or Regional Anaesthesia

With both local and regional anaesthesia, you are fully aware of what is going on during the operation and will remember it. With local anaesthesia, the anaesthetist blocks the pain signal where the nerve begins. For minor surgery on the foot, for example, you might have a few localized injections that will numb just the foot.

For more complex knee surgery, on the other hand, the anaesthetist might block pain responses from entire lower regions of the body by injecting an anaesthetic into the outer covering of the spinal column (called *epidural anaesthesia*).

With epidural anaesthesia, you have full feeling in your upper body and will be able to speak with the surgical staff during the actual procedure.

Which Anaesthesia Is Best?

The best anaesthesia will depend on a number of factors, including your general health, the procedure you are having and personal preference. A local or regional anaesthetic generally is less risky (see more about risks in Chapter 9), and you recover from it more quickly.

General anaesthesia is often necessary for long, complicated operations. Even so, doctors often use regional anaesthesia for such procedures as some joint replacement. Doing so may enable to you to be up and active more quickly, which may improve the odds of long-term success of the procedure.

QUESTIONS TO ASK YOUR DOCTOR ABOUT SURGERY

The decision to have surgery is a major one. You should collect as much information as possible about the operation before you agree to it. Here are some questions you may want to ask your doctor and the surgeon to better understand the surgical procedure.

You may find it helpful to talk to someone with your type of arthritis who has already had the operation you are considering. (Your doctor may be able to refer you to another patient.) Some of the questions listed below might be appropriate to ask that person, too. Remember: every person and every operation is different. Your operation may not go exactly as another person's, even if your situations are similar.

- What other kinds of treatment could I have instead of surgery? How successful might those treatments be?

- Can you explain this surgical procedure, step by step?

- How long does this surgery typically take?

- May I have this procedure on an out-patient basis?

- What are the risks involved in the surgery? How likely are these risks?

- How can I avoid blood transfusions? What other options are there?

- What type of anaesthesia will be used? What are the risks of anaesthesia?

- How much improvement can I expect from the operation?

- Will more surgery be necessary? After what period of time?

- If I choose to undergo this operation, will you contact my GP? Will my doctor be involved in my hospital stay? If so, in what way?

- Do you have a special interest or experience in arthritis surgery?

- What is your experience doing this type of surgery?

- Can you give me the name of someone else who has undergone this surgery and who would talk to me about it?

- Is an exercise programme recommended before and after the operation?

- Must I stop taking – or increase the dosage of – any of my medications before surgery?

- What happens if I delay surgery? Even for a few months?

- What are the risks if I don't have the surgery?

If you decide to proceed with surgery, here are some questions you will want to ask your doctor or surgeon. If you are having the operation as a private patient and you have health insurance, check on your coverage for surgery, rehabilitation and aftercare, including follow-up visits.

- How long will I need to stay in the hospital after having the surgery?

- How much pain is involved? Will I receive medication for it? What kind of pain should I expect? How long will this pain last?

- How long do I have to stay in bed?

- When will I start physiotherapy? Will I need home or outpatient therapy?

- Will I need to arrange for some assistance at home? If so, for how long?

- Will I need any special equipment for my home? Will I need to make any modifications to my home?

- What medications will I need for my recovery? How long will I need to take them?

- What limits will there be on my activities – driving, using the toilet, climbing stairs, bending, eating, having sex?

- How often will I have follow-up visits with you?

Complications and
Side Effects

9

CHAPTER 9:

COMPLICATIONS AND SIDE EFFECTS

As with any medical treatment, there are benefits and drawbacks to arthritis treatment. Every medication or surgical procedure involves an element of risk. Making optimal treatment decisions for your particular condition requires understanding as much as you can about those risks as well as the potential benefits of the treatment.

Before doctors prescribe a drug or recommend an operation, they consider what is called the risk/benefit ratio. That is, they estimate the risk of having the treatment and then compare that risk to the treatment's potential benefits. In other words, they weigh the potential risks of having a treatment against the risks of not having it. For example, if you had mild arthritis that caused only occasional pain and stiffness, your doctor would not be likely to prescribe a drug

that causes severe side effects in even 10 per cent of people who take it. In that case, the drug's potential risks clearly outweigh any benefits you might achieve from it.

On the other hand, if you have severe arthritis that is destroying your joints, or if you have a disease like lupus that is causing potentially life-threatening organ damage, even a certainty of some adverse effects might be preferable to not taking an otherwise helpful drug.

In most cases, the risk/benefit ratio is not so dramatic or clear-cut. In many cases, your doctor will rely largely on your judgement in the treatment process. After all, much of arthritis treatment involves judgement calls. Who can make those calls better than the person affected by them?

MEDICATION LABELLING

All medications come with instructions on how to take them. Medications that can be obtained only with a doctor's prescription must also be accompanied by more detailed information on what is called the 'patient information leaflet'. You should always read this leaflet before you begin taking a new medication; although your doctor will have taken into consideration your individual needs and other medications that you are taking, it is possible that there is a small, relevant, detail that was overlooked – in which case you will need to check with your doctor before taking the new drug.

DRUG RISKS

It's often said that anything strong enough to help is strong enough to harm. Any time you interfere with one bodily process to produce a desired effect, there's the chance that you'll produce a not-so-desirable effect somewhere else in the body. For example, a drug that suppresses your immune system so that it doesn't damage your joints may render your immune system less effective at fighting bacteria and viruses. The possible result: susceptibility to infection. A drug that suppresses the inflammation-causing, hormone-like substances called prostaglandins may suppress similar substances that protect the stomach lining from digestive juices. The possible result: stomach ulcers and bleeding.

Almost every medication – even the so-called natural ones – is associated with some type of side effect. Many side effects resolve on their own, with time. Others require prompt attention by your doctor. Still others are minor and may be necessary to live with if you are to receive the drugs' benefits.

If you experience any problems, no matter how minor, that you attribute to your medications, it's always best to talk to your doctor. Depending on your reaction, the doctor may choose to adjust your dose, recommend measures to ease the side effects, switch you to another medication or advise you to bear with it.

For a listing of commonly used arthritis medications and side effects associated with them, see pages 73–85. Keep in mind that not all people taking these drugs will experience these side effects. But any potential side effect at least warrants a call to your doctor or pharmacist. With medications, conventional wisdom applies: better safe than sorry.

With some exceptions, treatment for most forms of arthritis is not a life-and-death matter. Rather, it's an issue of quality of life. Are you willing to undergo the pain of surgery and a small risk of complications to be able to climb steps again or play on the floor with your grandchildren? Are you willing to put up with some medication-related nausea in return for the relief from progression of your arthritis that medication provides? Are you willing to undergo regular injections of medication and have regular blood tests to monitor the effects of a medication in order to lessen your chances of deformity or the need for surgery 10 years from now? These are the likely scenarios you'll be facing as you work with your doctor to determine your own risk/benefit ratio.

MINIMIZING YOUR RISK

Although some risk is inherent in any type of treatment you pursue, there are things you can do to minimize treatment risks, including the following:

Tell your doctor what medications you're taking. If your doctor prescribes a new medication, be sure to list all of the medications you are taking. If you are seeing more than one doctor for different medical conditions, it's possible that the doctor who treats your arthritis doesn't know about medications your other doctors have prescribed. Even if your doctor has noted such medications, it can't hurt to mention them again.

Let your doctor know if you are taking any over-the-counter medications, nutritional supplements or herbal remedies. Any of these agents has the potential to interact with or add to the effects of medications that your doctor prescribes. For example, if your doctor prescribes a non-steroidal anti-inflammatory drug, such as ibuprofen or naproxen, and you are already taking an over-the-counter brand-name NSAID, such as *Advil* or *Motrin*, you could be setting yourself up for side effects, including gastric ulcers.

In some cases, a potential drug interaction may be reason enough for your doctor to prescribe a different drug for you. On the other hand, if potential benefits of the new drug (remember the risk/benefit ratio) are great enough to risk a potential reaction, the doctor may simply want to monitor you more closely so that any adverse effects can be caught early and, if necessary, one of the drugs can be discontinued.

Consider your lifestyle habits. If your doctor asks if you smoke or drink, answer truthfully. If you aren't asked, offer the information. Lifestyle habits can make a difference in how medications work and can influence your risk of side effects. For example, having three or more drinks a day and taking paracetamol could increase your risk of liver damage, and the same amount of alcohol could cause stomach bleeding in people taking NSAIDs. Since alcohol can increase the risk of liver damage from methotrexate therapy, most rheumatologists advise patients taking methotrexate to forego alcohol altogether or to limit their intake to only a small amount.

Consider your health risks. Health problems, such as kidney, liver or heart disease, ulcers, clotting disorders or cancer may influence your doctor's decision to recommend surgery or prescribe a particular medication. Many of these problems can be solved by prescribing a different medication or monitoring you carefully for the first signs of an adverse effect.

For example, a woman who has had breast cancer or who has a family history of breast cancer may not be able to take oestrogen replacement hormone, the most common preventive treatment for osteoporosis. Oestrogen has the potential to cause a recurrence or worsening of cancer. On the

AVOIDING MEDICAL MISTAKES

A person diagnosed with arthritis – or, in fact, just about any disease – has a rapidly expanding array of treatment options. Today's technology enables doctors to manage and treat disease better than at any time in history. Such advances are not without a price. Increasing numbers of medications and medical procedures – along with increasingly busy and rushed medical staffs trying to keep up with and administer them all – can lead to problems.

By being alert to problems that could occur and taking a role in your health care, you can reduce the chance of a potentially dangerous mistake. Here are some things you can do:

- Be sure you get the right drug. Because drugs designed for entirely different purposes can have names that sound or look alike, it's important that you make sure you are getting the right drug. If you have any doubt about what your doctor is prescribing, ask for the drug's name and its spelling (doctors' handwriting on prescription pads is notoriously hard to read). When you get your prescription filled, make sure you have the medication your doctor prescribed. Ask your pharmacist to confirm your prescription.

- Read medication labels. Always read and follow the directions on your prescription label. Problems can occur if you don't take a medication exactly as prescribed. Included with every prescription medication is a 'patient information leaflet' with more extensive information about taking your drug. Read this leaflet and ask your pharmacist or doctor if you have any questions.

- Carefully reading – and heeding – labels on over-the-counter medications is essential. If you cannot understand the instructions, ask the pharmacist to explain them.

- If possible, choose a high-volume hospital. If you are undergoing joint surgery, one of the best ways to increase the odds of its success is to find a surgeon and a hospital who perform many procedures of the particular operation you will have.

- Take notes – or a friend. If you have difficulty remembering exactly what your doctor said once you leave the office, take notes. Another option is to take a friend or family member with you to your appointments. When it comes to comprehending and remembering important information, the old saying probably is right – two heads are better than one.

other hand, her doctor might prescribe one of the newer nonhormonal treatments for osteoporosis. Similarly, a person who has had ulcers probably wouldn't be a good candidate for traditional non-steroidal anti-inflammatory drugs, which can increase ulcer risk. However, there are medications, such as COX-2 inhibitors, that your doctor can prescribe to reduce pain and inflammation, and decrease ulcer risk.

Take your medication as prescribed. Adverse effects are more likely and a medication's benefits may be hampered if you don't take it exactly as prescribed. In general, it's best to take medications with a full glass of water. Be sure to ask your doctor or pharmacist about the best way to take your medication.

Some medications should be taken with food. Having a few crackers or a slice of bread, if not a full meal, can help reduce stomach upset associated with many drugs, but some drugs must be taken on an empty stomach to work. Others should not be taken with particular foods. If you have any doubts about how to take your medication, ask your doctor or the pharmacist filling the prescription. It is always a good idea to read carefully any written material provided with your medications.

Don't think that if one capsule helps a little, two or three ought to help a lot. Taking more than your prescribed dose of any medication can be dangerous.

If the medication you are taking is in liquid form, be sure to get a special measuring dropper or spoon to get the right dosage. The teaspoon you use for your morning cereal may be larger or smaller than an actual measuring spoon.

SURGERY RISKS & PREVENTION

Each year, joint replacement surgery gives many people the ability to move without pain for the first time in years, but it is not without risks. Here are some of the most common risks that you should be aware of before proceeding with joint surgery.

Blood clots. Joint surgery in general, and hip replacement in particular, carries the risk of blood-clot formation in the veins of the legs or the pelvis. While the clot is not dangerous in these areas, if it breaks loose and travels through the bloodstream to the lungs or another organ, it can cause organ damage, stroke or even death.

Prevention: With proper precautions, the risk of dangerous blood clots is slight. Preventive measures include the use of elasticated stockings as prescribed by your doctor, use of blood-thinning medications and getting out of bed and moving around as soon as advised by your doctor. Clots are most likely to form in your body while you are lying still in bed.

Infection. There is the potential for infection with all surgical procedures. With

Let your doctor know if you experience any side effects. If you experience any problems that you attribute to a medication or you suspect that problems may be related to your medication, consult your doctor. The doctor may choose to change your medication dose, advise you to wait out the problem or change the type of medicine.

total joint replacement, that risk exists mainly at the time of the surgery but, very rarely, afterwards, as well. Any infection that enters the body through a cut or, rarely, a dental procedure has the potential to travel to and settle in the replaced joint.

Prevention: Antibiotics used to be given to people undergoing surgery but this practice has been discontinued because the potential benefits were outweighed by the likelihood of adverse effects.

Joint Dislocation. When you have the ball-and-socket joint of the hip replaced, there is a slight risk that the ball of the prosthetic hip will slip out of the prosthetic socket. This risk is highest in the weeks just after surgery.

Prevention: To minimize the risk of a dislocation, it's important that you not bend your hip farther than a right (90-degree) angle. Twisting and crossing your legs also could put your new hip at risk. Speak to your surgeon about any particular exercises you should do or avoid to protect your hip.

Nerve Injury. In extremely rare cases, the main nerve that supplies the leg may be damaged during hip replacement surgery. The result may be difficulty moving the foot up and down or feelings of pins and needles in the affected leg.

Prevention: Although there is nothing you can do to prevent nerve damage, in the rare event that this occurs, it helps to know that such damage usually heals on its own, restoring full movement and feeling to the leg.

Loosening. Although loosening of the prosthesis is, perhaps, the most common risk of joint replacement, it doesn't usually occur until at least 10 years after you have had the operation.

Prevention: Aside from improved surgical techniques and materials, there is probably no way to prevent loosening. However, it's important that you report to your doctor any unusual pain around the replaced joint – particularly after the incision has healed. Pain can be a sign that the joint has loosened and further surgery is necessary to correct the problem. Because not all joint loosening is painful, doctors may order periodic X-rays following surgery to make sure that the new joint is firmly in place.

Never stop taking a medication without first speaking to your doctor. If you're taking high doses of corticosteroid medications, for example, or have been taking even a small dose over a long period of time, your doctor will need to wean you off of the medication. Stopping 'cold turkey' can cause serious side effects, including a flare of the disease you are trying to control, fever, low blood pressure, or the inability to eat or even function.

When you collect your prescription, each item will have a 'patient information leaflet' giving you information about how to take the drug and any side effects associated with it. Read over the leaflet and become familiar with any potential side effects that warrant medical attention.

Follow doctor's orders. Just as you must follow a medication prescription precisely, it's important that you do as your doctor advises. (In fact, the doctor's advice concerning a medication should supersede what you see on the medication label.) If he says not to climb stairs for two weeks after surgery, for example, don't climb stairs three days later. You could be setting yourself up for problems.

Beware of medical errors. Many problems with arthritis treatment are not inherent with the treatment, but are the result of medical errors. Taking the wrong medication for your condition or having the wrong joint operated on are obvious examples of serious medical errors, but they are not the only ones. By using caution and taking an active role in your health care, you can help reduce your risk of errors. For more advice on protecting yourself, see 'Avoiding Medical Mistakes' on page 109.

Other Ways to Ease Symptoms

10

CHAPTER 10:
OTHER WAYS TO EASE SYMPTOMS

Although arthritis medications (and, in certain cases, surgery) can improve pain, reduce swelling, prevent or, in the case of surgery, correct, deformity, they are not the whole solution. Far from it. There are many other things your doctor or other health professional can do for you and, even more importantly, that you can do for yourself.

In this chapter, we'll discuss some of the many methods – beyond medication and surgery – you may find helpful in easing the pain, stiffness and other symptoms of arthritis. Some of these – such as using hot and cold – you can begin right now at home. For others, you'll need the help of a health-care professional. And, if you are considering significant changes in your diet or exercise level, it's always a good idea to first consult your doctor.

EXERCISE

One of the best things you can do for yourself, whether or not you have arthritis, is to get regular exercise. You don't have run a marathon or bench-press your body weight to see the benefits of exercise. Something as simple as walking, gardening, raking leaves or doing aquarobics can help ease pain, stiffness and joint mobility problems.

Regular exercise has a number of benefits for people with arthritis. It can help you:

- Keep your joints moving, which increases their range of motion and helps ease stiffness;
- Strengthen muscles that support the joint, lightening the stressful load that fragile joints must bear;
- Keep bones strong and healthy, which reduces your risk of osteoporosis;
- Perform your daily activities more easily and, perhaps, maintain your independence until late in life, despite arthritis;
- Maintain your weight or lose weight, which can lessen stress on weight-bearing joints such as the hip and knee;
- Increase your energy and improve your sleep, both of which can be affected adversely by a chronic, painful disease like arthritis;
- Ease pain, by prompting your body to produce its own natural painkillers called endorphins;
- Improve your self-esteem, by showing you that you can be strong and active, despite arthritis;
- Make you healthier, by reducing your risk of such problems as heart disease, lung disease and certain cancers.

A regular exercise programme should consist of three types of exercise:
- Range-of-movement exercises, which keep your joints flexible, may involve bending, stretching or swaying.

- Strengthening (isometric) exercises, in which a force is applied to a resistant object. An example would be placing both palms together, upright, in front of you (as if you are praying) and pressing them against each other. Isometric exercises can be helpful in strengthening muscles that support arthritic joints.
- Aerobic or endurance exercises, which involve sustained use of large muscles and increased heart rate, will strengthen your heart and lungs. Aerobic exercise includes dancing, fast walking, swimming and jogging.

If your arthritis involves your hips, knees or the joints of your feet, it's best to avoid jarring exercises, such as high-impact (or 'regular') aerobics, running or jogging. For most people with arthritis, swimming, low-impact aerobics, walking, weightlifting, riding a stationary cycle or taking part in an aquarobics programme are safe and beneficial. The Arthritis Care booklet *Fit for Life* includes exercises that are suitable for people with arthritis.

Sample Exercises for Arthritis

Here are some sample exercises for general flexibility and strengthening that you can use to warm up or cool down. Try these exercises along with an aerobic exercise routine (such as walking or swimming) approved by your doctor. Note the precautions, if any, and choose the exercises that are best for you, depending on which areas of your body are painful. Always check with your doctor

before beginning any new exercise programme or routine, and describe what form of exercise you are considering. These suggested exercises are based on the US Arthritis Foundation's PACE (People with Arthritis Can Exercise) programme.

In addition to aerobic exercises such as walking, swimming or bicycling, many people with arthritis find benefit in gentle exercise alternatives, such as yoga, tai chi or *qi gong*. For some, the appeal of these alternatives is the ease and gentleness of the movements and the fact that they can be done in a small space with no special clothing or equipment. For others, these alternatives add variety to their exercise programme. More information is on page 131.

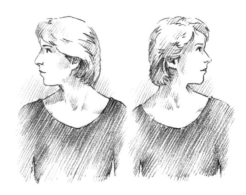

1. CHIN TUCKS

PULL YOUR CHIN BACK AS IF TO MAKE A DOUBLE CHIN. KEEP YOUR HEAD STRAIGHT – DON'T LOOK DOWN. HOLD THREE SECONDS. THEN RAISE YOUR NECK STRAIGHT UP AS IF SOMEONE WAS PULLING STRAIGHT UP ON YOUR HAIR.

2. HEAD TURNS (ROTATION)

TURN YOUR HEAD TO LOOK OVER YOUR SHOULDER. HOLD THREE SECONDS. RETURN TO THE CENTRE AND THEN TURN TO LOOK OVER YOUR OTHER SHOULDER. HOLD THREE SECONDS. REPEAT.

3. SHOULDER CIRCLES

LIFT BOTH SHOULDERS UP, MOVE THEM FORWARD, THEN DOWN AND BACK IN A CIRCLING MOTION. THEN LIFT BOTH SHOULDERS UP, MOVE THEM BACKWARD, THEN DOWN AND FORWARD IN A CIRCLING MOTION.

4. HEAD TILTS

FOCUS ON AN OBJECT IN FRONT OF YOU. TILT YOUR HEAD SIDEWAYS TOWARD YOUR RIGHT SHOULDER. HOLD THREE SECONDS. RETURN TO THE CENTRE AND TILT TOWARD YOUR LEFT SHOULDER. HOLD THREE SECONDS. DO NOT TWIST HEAD BUT CONTINUE TO LOOK FORWARD. DO NOT RAISE YOUR SHOULDER TOWARD YOUR EAR.

5. SHOULDER SHRUGS

(A) RAISE ONE SHOULDER, LOWER IT. THEN RAISE THE OTHER SHOULDER. BE SURE THE FIRST SHOULDER IS COMPLETELY RELAXED AND LOWERED BEFORE RAISING THE OTHER. (B) RAISE BOTH SHOULDERS UP TOWARD THE EARS. HOLD THREE SECONDS. RELAX. CONCENTRATE ON COMPLETELY RELAXING SHOULDERS AS THEY COME DOWN. DO NOT TILT THE HEAD OR BODY IN EITHER DIRECTION. DO NOT HUNCH YOUR SHOULDERS FORWARD OR PINCH SHOULDER BLADES TOGETHER.

6. FORWARD ARM REACH

RAISE ONE OR BOTH ARMS FORWARD AND UPWARD AS HIGH AS POSSIBLE. RETURN TO YOUR STARTING POSITION.

7. SELF BACK RUB

WHILE SEATED, SLIDE A FEW INCHES FORWARD FROM THE BACK OF YOUR CHAIR. SIT UP AS STRAIGHT AS POSSIBLE; DO NOT ROUND YOUR SHOULDERS. PLACE THE BACK OF YOUR HANDS ON YOUR LOWER BACK. SLOWLY MOVE THEM UPWARD UNTIL YOU FEEL A STRETCH IN YOUR SHOULDERS. HOLD THREE SECONDS, THEN SLIDE YOUR HANDS BACK DOWN. YOU CAN USE ONE HAND TO HELP THE OTHER. MOVE WITHIN THE LIMITS OF YOUR PAIN. DO NOT FORCE.

8. SHOULDER ROTATOR

SIT OR STAND AS STRAIGHT AS POSSIBLE. REACH UP AND PLACE YOUR HANDS ON THE BACK OF YOUR HEAD. (IF YOU CANNOT REACH YOUR HEAD, PLACE YOUR ARMS IN A 'MUSCLE MAN' POSITION WITH ELBOWS BENT IN A RIGHT ANGLE AND UPPER ARM AT SHOULDER LEVEL.) TAKE A DEEP BREATH IN. AS YOU BREATHE OUT, BRING YOUR ELBOWS TOGETHER IN FRONT OF YOU. SLOWLY MOVE ELBOWS APART AS YOU BREATHE IN.

9. DOOR OPENER

BEND YOUR ELBOWS AND HOLD THEM IN TO YOUR SIDES. YOUR FOREARMS SHOULD BE PARALLEL TO THE FLOOR. SLOWLY TURN FOREARMS AND PALMS TO FACE THE CEILING. HOLD THREE SECONDS AND THEN TURN PALMS SLOWLY TOWARD THE FLOOR.

10. BICEPS CURL

SIT IN A CHAIR, FEET ON THE FLOOR. HOLD A ONE-POUND WEIGHT IN YOUR RIGHT HAND, LETTING YOUR ARM HANG AT YOUR SIDE. BRING YOUR LEFT ARM ACROSS YOUR CHEST, RESTING THE BACK OF YOUR RIGHT ARM ON YOUR LEFT FIST. SLOWLY BEND YOUR ELBOW, TURNING YOUR RIGHT FOREARM TOWARD THE FRONT OF YOUR SHOULDER. YOUR PALM SHOULD BE FACING YOUR SHOULDER. PAUSE, THEN LOWER YOUR ARM TO THE COUNT OF THREE. REPEAT ON THE LEFT SIDE.

11. OVERHEAD TRICEPS

SIT IN A CHAIR, HOLDING A ONE-POUND WEIGHT IN YOUR RIGHT HAND. BRING YOUR RIGHT ARM ABOVE YOUR HEAD, STOPPING WHEN THE INSIDE OF YOUR ELBOW IS ABOVE YOUR RIGHT EAR. SUPPORT YOUR RIGHT UPPER ARM WITH YOUR LEFT HAND. SLOWLY BEND YOUR RIGHT ELBOW, LOWERING THE WEIGHT TO YOUR RIGHT SHOULDER. STRAIGHTEN YOUR ELBOW TO THE COUNT OF THREE, PAUSE, THEN LOWER IT BACK TO YOUR SHOULDER. REPEAT WITH THE LEFT ARM.

(THESE TWO EXERCISES ADAPTED FROM *ARTHRITIS TODAY*)

12. WRIST BEND

IF SITTING, REST HANDS AND FOREARMS ON THIGHS, TABLE, OR ARMS OF CHAIR. IF STANDING, BEND YOUR ELBOWS AND HOLD HANDS IN FRONT OF YOU, PALMS DOWN. LIFT PALMS AND FINGERS, KEEPING FOREARMS FLAT. HOLD THREE SECONDS. RELAX.

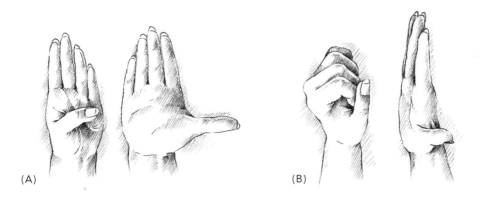

(A)   (B)

13. THUMB BEND AND FINGER CURL

(A) WITH HANDS OPEN AND FINGERS RELAXED, REACH THUMB ACROSS YOUR PALM AND TRY TO TOUCH THE BASE OF YOUR LITTLE FINGER. HOLD THREE SECONDS. STRETCH THUMB BACK OUT TO THE OTHER SIDE AS FAR AS POSSIBLE.

(B) MAKE A LOOSE FIST BY CURLING ALL YOUR FINGERS INTO YOUR PALM. KEEP YOUR THUMB OUT. HOLD FOR THREE SECONDS. THEN STRETCH YOUR FINGERS TO STRAIGHTEN THEM.

14. SIDE BENDS

WHILE STANDING, KEEP WEIGHT EVENLY ON BOTH HIPS WITH KNEES SLIGHTLY BENT. LEAN TOWARD THE RIGHT AND REACH YOUR FINGERS TOWARD THE FLOOR. HOLD THREE SECONDS. RETURN TO CENTRE AND REPEAT EXERCISE TOWARD THE LEFT. DO NOT LEAN FORWARD OR BACKWARD WHILE BENDING, AND DO NOT TWIST THE TORSO.

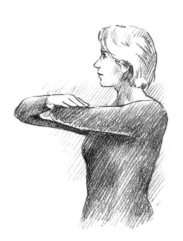  

15. TRUNK TWIST

PLACE YOUR HANDS ON YOUR HIPS, STRAIGHT OUT TO THE SIDE, CROSSED OVER YOUR CHEST, OR ON OPPOSITE ELBOWS. TWIST YOUR BODY AROUND TO LOOK OVER YOUR RIGHT SHOULDER. HOLD THREE SECONDS. RETURN TO THE CENTRE AND THEN TWIST TO THE LEFT. BE SURE YOU ARE TWISTING AT THE WAIST AND NOT AT YOUR NECK OR HIPS. NOTE: VARY THE EXERCISE BY HOLDING A BALL IN FRONT OF OR NEXT TO YOUR BODY.

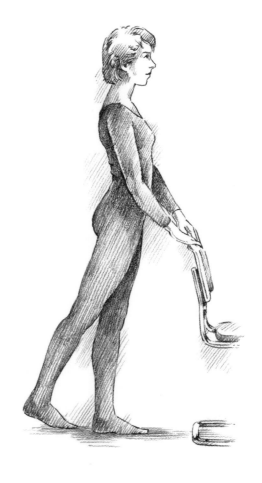

16. MARCH

STAND SIDEWAYS TO A CHAIR AND LIGHTLY GRASP THE BACK. IF YOU FEEL UNSTEADY, HOLD ONTO TWO CHAIRS OR FACE THE BACK OF THE CHAIR. ALTERNATE LIFTING YOUR LEGS UP AND DOWN AS IF MARCHING IN PLACE. GRADUALLY TRY TO LIFT KNEES HIGHER AND/OR MARCH FASTER.

17. BACK KICK

STAND STRAIGHT ON ONE LEG AND LIFT THE OTHER LEG BEHIND YOU. HOLD THREE SECONDS. TRY TO KEEP YOUR LEG STRAIGHT AS YOU MOVE IT BACKWARD. MOTION SHOULD OCCUR ONLY IN THE HIP (NOT THE WAIST). DO NOT LEAN FORWARD – KEEP YOUR UPPER BODY STRAIGHT. NOTE: YOU CAN ADD RESISTANCE BY USING A LARGE RUBBER EXERCISE BAND AROUND ANKLES.

18. SIDE LEG KICK
STAND NEAR A CHAIR, HOLDING IT FOR SUPPORT. STAND ON ONE LEG AND LIFT THE OTHER LEG OUT TO THE SIDE. HOLD THREE SECONDS AND RETURN YOUR LEG TO THE FLOOR. ONLY MOVE YOUR LEG AT THE TOP – DON'T LEAN TOWARD THE CHAIR. ALTERNATE LEGS.

19. HIP TURNS
STAND WITH LEGS SLIGHTLY APART, WITH YOUR WEIGHT ON ONE LEG AND THE HEEL OF YOUR OTHER FOOT LIGHTLY TOUCHING THE FLOOR. ROTATE YOUR WHOLE LEG FROM THE HIP SO THAT TOES AND KNEE POINT IN AND THEN OUT. DON'T ROTATE YOUR BODY – KEEP CHEST AND SHOULDERS FACING FORWARD. NOTE: IF YOU HAVE DIFFICULTY PUTTING WEIGHT ON ONE LEG, YOU CAN DO THIS EXERCISE BY SITTING AT THE EDGE OF A CHAIR WITH YOUR LEGS EXTENDED STRAIGHT IN FRONT AND YOUR HEELS RESTING ON THE FLOOR.

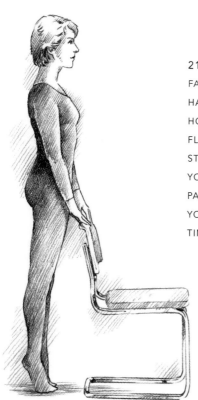

21. TIPTOE

FACE THE BACK OF A CHAIR AND REST YOUR HANDS ON IT. RISE AND STAND ON YOUR TOES. HOLD THREE SECONDS, THEN RETURN TO THE FLAT POSITION. TRY TO KEEP YOUR KNEES STRAIGHT (BUT NOT LOCKED). NOW STAND ON YOUR HEELS, RAISING YOUR TOES AND FRONT PART OF YOUR FOOT OFF THE GROUND. NOTE: YOU CAN DO THIS EXERCISE ONE FOOT AT A TIME.

20. SKIER'S SQUAT
(QUADRICEPS STRENGTHENER)

STAND BEHIND A CHAIR WITH YOUR HANDS LIGHTLY RESTING ON TOP OF THE CHAIR FOR SUPPORT. KEEP YOUR FEET FLAT ON THE FLOOR. KEEPING YOUR BACK STRAIGHT, SLOWLY BEND YOUR KNEES TO LOWER YOUR BODY A FEW INCHES. HOLD FOR THREE TO SIX SECONDS, THEN SLOWLY RETURN TO AN UPRIGHT POSITION.

22. CALF STRETCH

HOLD LIGHTLY TO THE BACK OF A CHAIR. BEND THE KNEE OF THE LEG YOU ARE NOT STRETCHING
SO THAT IT ALMOST TOUCHES THE CHAIR. PUT THE LEG TO BE STRETCHED BEHIND YOU, KEEPING
BOTH FEET FLAT ON THE FLOOR. LEAN FORWARD GENTLY, KEEPING YOUR BACK KNEE STRAIGHT.

23. CHEST STRETCH

STAND ABOUT TWO TO THREE FEET AWAY FROM A WALL AND PLACE YOUR HANDS OR FOREARMS ON THE WALL AT SHOULDER HEIGHT. LEAN FORWARD, LEADING WITH YOUR HIPS. KEEP YOUR KNEES STRAIGHT AND YOUR HEAD BACK. HOLD THIS POSITION FOR FIVE TO 10 SECONDS, THEN PUSH BACK TO STARTING POSITION. TO FEEL MORE STRETCH, PLACE YOUR HANDS FARTHER APART.

24. THIGH FIRMER AND KNEE STRETCH

SIT ON THE EDGE OF YOUR CHAIR OR LIE ON YOUR BACK WITH YOUR LEGS STRETCHED OUT IN FRONT AND YOUR HEELS RESTING ON THE FLOOR. TIGHTEN THE MUSCLE THAT RUNS ACROSS THE FRONT OF THE KNEE BY PULLING YOUR TOES TOWARD YOUR HEAD. PUSH THE BACK OF THE KNEE DOWN TOWARD THE FLOOR SO YOU ALSO FEEL A STRETCH AT THE BACK OF YOUR KNEE AND ANKLE. FOR A GREATER STRETCH, PUT YOUR HEEL ON A FOOTSTOOL AND LEAN FORWARD AS YOU PULL YOUR TOES TOWARD YOUR HEAD.

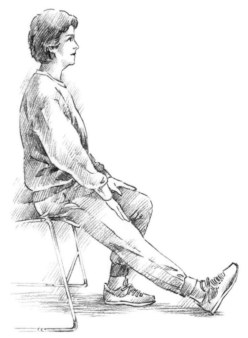

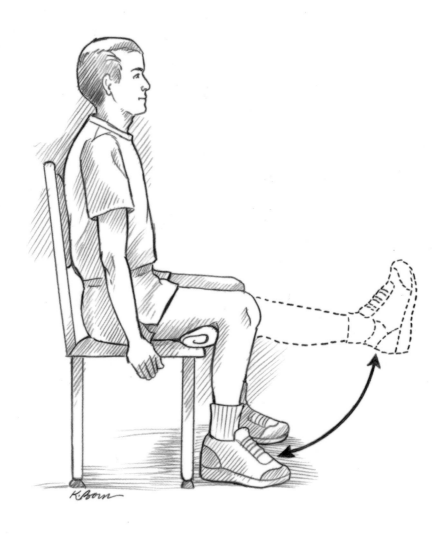

25. KNEE EXTENSION

SIT IN A CHAIR WITH YOUR FEET SHOULDER-WIDTH APART, KNEES DIRECTLY ABOVE THEM. PUT A
TOWEL UNDER YOUR KNEES FOR PADDING. WITH YOUR ARMS AT YOUR SIDES, RAISE YOUR RIGHT LEG
TO THE COUNT OF THREE UNTIL YOUR KNEE IS STRAIGHT (BUT NOT LOCKED). PAUSE, THEN LOWER
YOUR LEG TO THE COUNT OF THREE. REPEAT ON THE LEFT SIDE.

Yoga

Practised around the world, yoga is part of the traditional Indian healing system called Ayurveda. Although there are several branches of yoga practice, the form you're most probably familiar with is hatha yoga. Hatha yoga consists of balancing exercises and gentle stretches that condition the whole body.

Practising yoga daily can improve flexibility and balance and increase muscle strength. It can also help you relax. If you are interested in trying yoga, many colleges, community centres, day centres, health clubs and even workplaces offer yoga classes.

Before signing up for a yoga class, it's best to discuss it with your doctor. Some types of yoga are more strenuous than others. You need to find an instructor who is familiar with arthritis and who will be sensitive to your limitations if there are moves that you can't do comfortably. Once you have learned yoga from a competent instructor, you may want to practise with an instructional video. Your doctor, yoga instructor or physiotherapist may be able to recommend a good video that is appropriate for people with arthritis.

Tai Chi

Although its roots are in martial arts, tai chi is not confrontational. It consists of controlled movements that flow rhythmically into one long, graceful gesture. Research has shown that tai chi improves balance and reduces the risk of falling, which could be serious for a person with fragile bones and joints. At least one study has suggested that tai chi is safe for people with rheumatoid arthritis. Because of its gentle, graceful movements, it's a popular form of exercise for people with many different forms of arthritis. There are many more videos and books, along with classes locally, providing instruction in tai chi. Consult your health-care professional.

Qi Gong

Qi gong (pronounced chee kung) has been practised in Asia for more than 3,000 years to promote health and self-healing. There are several styles of qi gong, which involve meditation, breathing exercises and movements. In general, qi gong is less graceful than tai chi, and some styles are more active than others. Qi gong exercises can be practised by people of all ages and fitness levels. They can even be done from a bed or wheelchair.

Although qi gong has not been well studied for arthritis, in a 1998 study of fibromyalgia patients, those using qi gong with meditation reported improvement in depression, coping skills, pain and function.

If you have any questions about a particular exercise or would like an exercise programme suited to your particular condition and needs, consult a physiotherapist.

PHYSIOTHERAPY

Despite the proven and varied benefits of exercise, if you have arthritis, you should not begin an exercise programme without consulting your doctor – particularly if your arthritis has caused you to be sedentary for

AQUAROBICS

In addition to the ordinary exercises shown in this book, you might be able to attend aquarobics sessions at your local swimming pool or leisure centre. The buoyancy of the water helps support you as you exercise gently. Enquire at the local leisure centre to see if they offer this.

In some areas there might even be hydrotherapy that you could attend. For this the swimming pool has warm water and a trained therapist to help you to work through exercises, which are made easier by the warmth – just as you might find it easier to move your limbs while in the bath.

some time. Your doctor may want to give you a physical evaluation or refer you to a physiotherapist.

A physiotherapist (physio) is a health-care professional who helps people with arthritis by teaching them to do exercises designed to meet certain goals. Unlike a personal trainer, whose goal may be to help you firm your thighs and look better in a bathing suit, a physiotherapist's goal is to help you function better.

Physiotherapy generally begins with a complete assessment of the joints to determine range of motion and muscle strength. The physio may ask to see you walk and question you about any joints that are painful.

Once the assessment is complete, the physio will prescribe a programme of exercise to improve your joints' range of motion and increase the strength of muscles supporting arthritic joints. He or she may recommend a programme of aerobic exercise that will not damage your joints, and may prescribe devices to help address any particular problems you are having. These devices could include a crutch or cane to help you walk with an arthritic knee, or a shoe insert to ease

painful feet or compensate for a discrepancy in leg length, which may contribute to or be a result of arthritis.

If you have any kind of joint surgery, physiotherapy will probably be necessary to increase the strength of muscles that support the joint that was operated on and to help the joint – and you – function optimally afterwards.

You will probably want to consult your doctor about physiotherapy, because, in most cases, you will need a referral to consult a physio. To obtain physiotherapy paid for by the NHS, you will have to be referred by your surgeon or doctor. If your problem is relatively minor, a session or two with a physio may provide the information you need to begin an effective exercise programme. On the other hand, if your arthritis is severe and affects several joints, or if you are having major surgery such as total hip replacement, you may need regular, frequent sessions – at least for a while.

OCCUPATIONAL THERAPY

As with physiotherapy, the goal of occupational therapy is to help you function better with arthritis. Instead of exercise, occupational therapy focuses on different ways of doing things or using devices to help you manage specific household, self-care and job-related activities.

If arthritis makes it difficult for you to do such tasks as brush your teeth, shower, get dressed, drive a car, work on a computer or cook, an occupational therapist (OT) may help.

Similarly, if arthritis makes it difficult for you to pursue leisure activities, such as arts and crafts or photography, an OT may be able to recommend or devise new ways of holding a camera, carrying equipment, or cutting, gluing or painting craft projects.

An occupational therapist may recommend special devices – such as long-handled grabbers, spring-loaded scissors, built-up brush handles or keys, or computer arm rests – to help you with your activities. The OT may prescribe or design splints or braces to protect joints and hold them in proper position while you are working or resting.

Braces and splints

Braces and splints are devices used to support or stabilize a joint. Braces and splints are made from an array of materials, such as metal, plastic, cloth and mouldable foam. They may be used after surgery, for example, to hold a joint in position while it fuses following arthrodesis, or to support a replaced knee until the supporting muscles have been strengthened sufficiently to do the job through physiotherapy. In some cases, they are prescribed to stabilize a joint that is causing disability.

Splints and braces may be worn to position a joint in a way that helps prevent further irritation or injury to a joint or the soft tissues surrounding it. Wrist splints are commonly used for this purpose. Wrist splints may be especially helpful for people with rheumatoid arthritis in the wrist or with carpal tunnel syndrome, a condition in which the soft tissues in the wrist swell and compress the nerve running the length of the arm to the palm, causing numbness or tingling in the fingers.

Some people find it helpful to wear braces or splints during the day as they go about

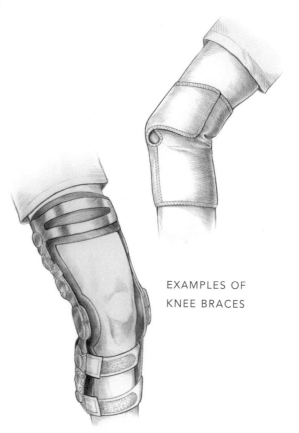

EXAMPLES OF
KNEE BRACES

their activities; others prefer to wear them at night to keep their joints from bending awkwardly while they sleep. Some people wear them 24 hours a day.

In most cases, your doctor or therapist prescribing the splint or brace will give you instructions on when to use it. Most health professionals advise not wearing a splint or brace around the clock unless specifically told to do so, because constantly holding a joint in one position long-term could potentially lead to permanently diminished range of motion.

Another type of splint, made for the fingers, can help prevent hand deformity. (Rarely, such splints may be made of silver-coloured metal and look more like jewellery than medical devices.) Ask your doctor or physiotherapist for information about finger splints.

Braces and splints can be ready-made or custom designed and made by a physio- or occupational therapist or an orthotist, a person who specializes in making braces, splints and similar devices.

JOINT PROTECTION

In the course of each day, sore, damaged joints are taxed by all of the activities you must perform just to maintain a home, prepare a meal, perform a job, practise good hygiene or complete your daily tasks. We stress our joints each time we walk, lift, grip, hold, twist, cut, write, reach, brush, bend or stir. By knowing how to protect our joints, however, we can use them in ways that avoid excess stress. Here are a few things you might try:

- **Pay attention to joint position.** This means using joints in the best way to avoid excess stress on them, such as using larger or stronger joints to carry things. For instance, you might carry bags by using your forearms or palms instead of your fingers.
- **Use assistive devices.** Devices, such as canes, crutches and walkers, can reduce stress on your hips and knees. Pencils and pens with built-up handles can protect finger joints and make it easier to write. Long handles and grabbers may spare shoulders when you need an item from a high shelf. Lightweight items, such as paper cups or plastic dishes, are easier to carry, and lightweight items, such as small, light vacuum cleaners, are easier to manoeuvre, making it easier to keep house.
- **Control your weight.** Excess pounds add excess stress to joints of the knees, hips and feet. If you have knee OA, losing weight may spare your joint some stress and reduce pain.

The Arthritis Care booklet *Talk About Pain* includes a section on splints, and its *Reaching Independence* has tips about household aids.

HOT AND COLD TREATMENTS

Heat and cold treatments are easy methods you can use at home to reduce the pain and stiffness of arthritis. Cold packs can numb the painful area and reduce inflammation and swelling. They are especially good for joint pain caused by a flare of arthritis. Heat, on the other hand, relaxes muscles and stimulates blood circulation.

Helpful Hints for Using Hot and Cold

Using heat and cold treatments can be an easy and effective way to reduce pain, inflammation and stiffness. There is a right way and a wrong way to do it. Follow the suggestions below to get the greatest benefits from your hot and cold treatment and to reduce the risk of harm to the skin and underlying tissue.

- Use heat or cold for only 15 to 20 minutes at a time.
- Avoid using treatments that are extremely hot or cold.
- Always put a towel between your skin and the hot or cold pack.
- Don't use creams, gels or lotions on your skin with a cold or hot treatment.
- To prevent burns, turn off your heating pad before going to sleep.
- Use an electric blanket or mattress pad. Turn it up before you get out of bed to help ease morning stiffness. Follow the directions on the blanket or pad carefully to ensure safety.
- Use a hot-water bottle to keep your feet, back or hands warm.
- Consult your doctor or physiotherapist before using cold packs if you have poor circulation, vasculitis or Raynaud's phenomenon.
- As with any treatment, follow the advice of your health-care professional when using these methods.

Heat and cold can be applied to joints in a number of ways. Cold may be applied with commercially available cold packs that can be placed in your freezer and refrozen, as needed. You can make your own cold pack by wrapping a towel round a bag of frozen peas or a sealable sandwich bag filled with ice.

Heat treatments may be dry or moist. Dry heat sources include heat lamps or heating pads. Moist heat sources include warm baths, washcloths soaked in warm water and paraffin baths, which involve placing the affected joint, usually those of the hand or wrist, into a container of melted paraffin, which adheres to skin, and provides warmth.

Before using either hot or cold, be sure your skin is dry and free from cuts and sores. If you have visible skin damage, don't use cold or heat, especially paraffin baths. After using heat or cold, carefully dry the skin and check for

benefits of applying heat can include muscle relaxation and decreased pain and stiffness. Immersing your body in warm water is an especially good way to apply heat to many parts of the body all at once.

By allowing your muscles to relax, warm water also provides an excellent environment for exercise. Water may also act as resistance to help build muscle strength during exercise, and the buoyancy of water supports the joints, making exercise easier and allowing you to move in ways that you can't when out of the water.

If you find that pain and stiffness are worst in the morning, soaking and performing gentle exercises in a bath, whirlpool bath or warm shower upon arising can help you get ready to take on your daily activities. If pain increases throughout the day, a warm soak before bedtime might make it easier to get to sleep. Be aware that some people find soaking before bedtime to be stimulating, and this practice keeps them awake. If that's the case with you, limit your use of warm water to the afternoon and early evening hours.

purplish-red skin or rash, which may indicate the treatment was too strong. Allow your skin to return to normal temperature and colour before using heat or cold again.

For some helpful tips on using heat and cold safely, see 'Helpful Hints for Using Hot and Cold' on page 135.

WATER THERAPY

You know how good it can feel to soak in a warm bath, especially when your joints are aching, your muscles are cramping and you're feeling downright miserable. It turns out that being in water not only feels good, it's good for you too. Studies have shown that the

MASSAGE

Aside from medication, surgery and physiotherapy, massage may be one of the most widely used arthritis treatments. Although it is not well studied for arthritis, many people report significant benefits in terms of pain and relaxation.

Although there are many forms of massage, the type most people are familiar with is Swedish massage, a full-body treatment that

How To Do Self-Massage

You bump your elbow or close a cabinet door on your finger. What is your first response? If you're like most people, you probably rub the painful area. And when you do, it probably feels a little better, at least for a while.

With a little instruction and practice, a similar type of rubbing – called self-massage – can help relieve the pain of arthritis. Your hands can benefit, too, because they'll get a workout during the process.

If you'd like try self-message, here are a few suggestions for getting started:

- **Get professional advice.** A massage therapist can show you some techniques to use.

- **Warm up before you start.** A warm bath or shower can relax you, make your hands more supple and improve circulation.

- **Create a healing environment.** Find a warm, quiet place without distractions. For some people, music can help create a relaxing environment.

- **Use a little lotion.** Using a little oil or lotion can help your hands glide over your body. A lightly scented massage oil can be soothing to your body – and your spirit.

- **Consider an appliance.** If your hands are affected to the point where self-massage is painful or impossible, or if limited range of motion makes it difficult to reach painful joints, try a vibrating massage appliance. Be sure to follow the manufacturer's instructions and limit the use to a few minutes at a time.

- **Be firm, but gentle.** Use firm, gentle strokes and pressure, especially over the joints where skin and muscle layers are thin. Pressing too hard can irritate your skin and the joint or muscle you are trying to help.

involves stroking or kneading the top layers of muscles with oils or lotions. Other forms of massage include:

- Deep tissue massage, in which the massage therapist uses fingers, thumbs and elbows to put strong pressure on deep muscle or tissue layers to relieve chronic tension.

- Neuromuscular massage (also called trigger point therapy), in which the therapist applies pressure with the fingers to certain spots that can trigger pain in other parts of the body.

- Myofascial release, a type of massage that involves applying slow, steady pressure to

THE GOUT EXCEPTION

Although most forms of arthritis are probably influenced very little by the types of foods you eat, there is one notable exception: gout. Gout occurs when a bodily waste product called uric acid builds up in the blood and is deposited as crystals in the joints, causing joints to become hot, swollen and excruciatingly painful.

While medication is needed to treat gout in many people, proper diet and weight loss can help keep the disease under control. If you have gout, your doctor will probably advise you to limit alcohol consumption to no more than one or two drinks a day and to avoid such foods as organ meats (e.g. kidneys, heart), sardines, anchovies and fish roe.

It's also important that you stay well hydrated, by drinking two litres (about 8 glasses) of non-alcoholic, decaffeinated liquids per day.

relieve tension in the fascia, or thin tissue around the muscles.

Although massage therapy generally is safe, as with any therapy, there are some precautions. For example, you should never have massage on an inflamed joint or on skin that is broken or infected. Let your massage therapist know if you have other health problems, including circulatory problems.

If you think you might be interested in massage, consult your doctor, physiotherapist or other health professional who may be able to refer you to a massage therapist with experience in your particular condition.

DIET AND WEIGHT LOSS

Although anecdotal reports of food-allergy-induced arthritis abound, research has shown that food sensitivities rarely play a role in arthritis. That's not to say that what you eat doesn't matter. For optimal health – whether you have arthritis or not – it's important to consume a healthy diet that is rich in vitamins and minerals and low in saturated fats and calories.

Arthritis Care's booklet *Food for Thought* is a guide to diet for people with arthritis. It includes information on supplements. Consuming plenty of calcium-rich products, including fortified juices and low-fat dairy products, keeps bones strong, reducing your risk of osteoporosis.

In addition, people with inflammatory forms of arthritis, such as rheumatoid arthritis or ankylosing spondylitis, may benefit from changing the types of fats and oils in their diets. Safflower, sunflower and corn oil, as well as fats in meat and poultry, may contribute to inflammation; olive, rapeseed, linseed oils and cold water fish oils may help reduce inflammation.

Some people believe that certain foods make their arthritis worse. If you suspect a food is aggravating your arthritis, it can't hurt to eliminate that food from your diet for a few weeks and observe what happens. But doctors advise against cutting out entire groups of foods (such as all dairy products, all green vegetables or all fruits, for example), which could leave you with nutritional deficiencies. It's also important that you don't stop taking your medications, even if you believe you have eliminated a problematic food. Because arthritis can come and go, it's difficult to be certain if a food really is having an effect on your disease. Neglecting your medical treatment while pursuing problem foods can leave you vulnerable to a flare of arthritis or irreparable joint damage.

Whether or not diet has a direct effect on arthritis, a healthy diet can help you manage your weight and take off and keep off excess pounds that are hard on your weight-bearing joints. A proper diet can reduce your risk of cardiovascular disease and cancer, either of which could be devastating, especially if you have arthritis.

The Food Guide Pyramid

As we learned, losing pounds if necessary, or maintaining your weight if it is appropriate, requires a balanced lifestyle of regular exercise and proper diet. Consult your doctor or a registered dietitian if you need advice on losing weight. A good general guideline for a balanced daily food intake is the US Food Guide Pyramid, a visual diagram of that government agency's recommended healthy diet. The foods at the base of the pyramid should make up the bulk of your diet, the foods in the middle should be eaten in moderate quantities, and the foods at the very top of the pyramid should be eaten sparingly. The suggested diet emphasizes building your daily food intake on a base of low-fat, high-fibre breads, grains and complex carbohydrates; eating at least five portions a day of fruit and vegetables; including moderate amounts of lean proteins such as fish, meats and poultry; eating moderate servings of dairy products, which add calcium; and eating small amounts of fats, sugars and oils.

FATS, OILS, SUGARS

MILK, YOGURT, CHEESE

MEAT, POULTRY, FISH, DRY BEANS, EGGS, NUTS

VEGETABLES

FRUIT

BREAD, CEREAL, RICE, PASTA

FOLLOWING THE FOOD GUIDE PYRAMID CAN HELP YOU EAT A WELL-BALANCED DIET THAT CONSISTS PRIMARILY OF GRAINS, FRUITS AND VEGETABLES.

TRANSCUTANEOUS ELECTRICAL NERVE STIMULATION (TENS)

If your pain is severe and doesn't respond to medication or other non-medication therapies, and if it is localized to the spine or a single hip or knee, you may be a candidate for transcutaneous electrical nerve stimulation (TENS). As its name suggests, TENS is a technique that uses electrical stimulation to the nerves to block pain signals to the brain.

To administer TENS, electrodes will be placed on your skin near the painful area. They are attached to a small battery-operated box that emits low-level electrical energy. When the box emits its energy, you will receive a low-level shock that gives a tingling sensation and, if all goes well, some temporary relief from your pain. You will probably be given TENS by a physiotherapist, and you can also buy a TENS machine to use at home if this is appropriate for you. They are often available at chemist shops and cost about £60.

TENS doesn't work for everyone, and it is not appropriate for widespread pain. For some people, however, it provides at least temporary relief when it may seem that nothing else helps.

STRESS REDUCTION

In addition to the disease process, one of the biggest factors in arthritis pain is stress. Being in pain is stressful and being under stress can add to your pain. Because stress and pain go hand in hand, there is not a clear line between stress-reduction therapies and pain-reduction therapies. Anything you do to ease pain will help ease the stress, and anything you do to ease stress has the potential to ease your pain.

Although this chapter primarily discusses methods used for pain relief, some of these methods may work equally well for stress. For example, you may get – or give yourself – a massage as a way to ease pain and relax. Similarly, you may take a walk or a yoga class or soak in a warm bath to relieve stress and pain.

In Chapter 11, we'll discuss some activities and techniques you may pursue purely for relaxation. These activities may have the pleasant side effect of easing your pain.

Reducing Stress

11

CHAPTER 11: REDUCING STRESS

Nobody lives completely free from stress. In our fast-paced, have-it-all, do-it-all society, stress is a daily problem in many people's lives. When you feel stressed, your muscles become tense. Muscle tension can, in turn, increase your pain and limit your physical abilities, which can lead to depression. A vicious cycle of stress, pain, limited/lost abilities and depression may develop.

If you have arthritis, you're not immune to the same kind of stressors that affect everyone else. You will probably have some stresses that healthy people don't, such as making important treatment decisions, needing to rely on other people more than in the past, living with pain, making changes in your lifestyle and favourite activities because of limited abilities, or seeing your appearance changed by the effects of the disease. None of these stressors is easy to deal with, but learning how to manage your stress can make it a little easier and help break the stress–pain–limited/lost abilities–depression cycle.

If stress is affecting your life and your health, learning to relax may be one of the most helpful things you can do for yourself, but you must understand that relaxing involves more than just sitting back and watching TV for an hour or two before bedtime. It involves becoming aware of what causes you stress and what you can do to eliminate the stressor or change your reaction to it.

For example, if you have young children and having a messy house causes you to be stressed, teaching your children to clean up after themselves, limiting their number of toys and enlisting your spouse to clean up may help eliminate the stressor (a messy house). Changing your reaction to the stressor would be admitting to yourself that children make messes and insisting on a spotless house is not only unrealistic, but may also needlessly affect your health.

The first step in easing stress in your life is to recognize what causes you stress and how you respond to it. Although that sounds obvious, the causes of stress aren't always clear-cut. For example, you may attribute a stress-related stomachache to something you ate. Or you may think that a stress headache was caused by a medication, sinus congestion or any number of factors – until you notice that you get one every time you face a stressful situation. To help yourself identify your stressors and your responses to them, try keeping a diary using the model on page 145.

STRESS REDUCTION AND RELAXATION TECHNIQUES

As troublesome as stress is, something as simple as taking time to daydream or write in a journal can help reduce your stress – and may even have beneficial effects on your pain and your disease.

Keeping a Stress Diary

An important first step to eliminating stress is to identify what causes it and how you

A Sample Stress Diary

Date	Time	Cause of Stress	Physical Symptoms	Emotional Symptoms
18/4	7 a.m.	Getting kids off to school	Fast heartbeat, tightness of neck	Feel rushed, disorganized
18/4	8 a.m.	Stuck in traffic	Headache, heart beating faster, legs aching	Frustrated, angry at being late
18/4	9 a.m.	Meeting presentation	Fast heartbeat, dry throat, clammy palms	Anxious, nervous
18/4	6:35 p.m.	Cooking dinner	Headache, jaw tightening	Feel overwhelmed
18/4	8 p.m.	Watching TV with kids	Fast heartbeat	Angry; kids argued to watch cop shows

respond, physically and emotionally. By keeping a daily stress diary, you should start to discover a pattern of stressors and symptoms. You will see how a stressor causes both physical and emotional reactions. Then you can begin to address your stress by using some of the techniques in this book. See 'A Sample Stress Diary' on this page for an example you can follow.

Relaxation Techniques

Relaxation techniques help you deal more calmly and effectively with life's stresses. Following are a few common techniques that might help:

Deep breathing. To practise deep breathing, sit in a comfortable chair with your feet on the floor and your arms at your sides. Close your eyes and breathe in deeply, saying to yourself, 'I am . . .', then slowly breathe out, while saying, '. . . relaxed.'

Continue to breathe slowly, silently repeating something to yourself such as, 'My hands . . . are warm; my feet . . . are warm; my breathing . . . is deep and smooth; my heartbeat . . . is calm and steady; I feel calm . . . and at peace.'

Always coordinate the words you say with your breathing.

Distraction. Distraction involves training your mind to focus on something other than your stress. This does not mean that you will ignore your stress, only that you choose not to dwell on it. When you anticipate a stressful situation, such as driving in heavy traffic or having a joint injection, prepare yourself for the stress and how you will handle it. Make plans for what you will do once the stressful situation has passed, because although it may seem at the time as if the problem will last forever, it will pass. By thinking of something else, you can take your mind off what is causing you stress.

Guided imagery. Like distraction, guided imagery helps take your focus off your stress. To practise guided imagery, close your eyes, take a deep breath and hold it for several seconds. Breathe out slowly, feeling your body relax as you do. Think about a place you have been where you felt safe and comfortable. Imagine it in as much detail as possible. Imagine the sounds you heard – of waves against the sand, seagulls calling overhead, children laughing on the beach. Imagine the way it felt, smelled and tasted – the saltwater on your lips, the soft sand beneath your feet, the sea breeze blowing through your hair. Recapture the positive feelings you had when you were there and keep them in your mind. Take several deep breaths and enjoy feeling calm and peaceful before you open your eyes.

Progressive relaxation. Progressive relaxation is a therapy in which the body's muscles, from head to toe, are progressively tensed and then relaxed. Progressive relaxation is a popular form of stress management.

To practise progressive relaxation, first close your eyes and take a deep breath, filling your chest and breathing all the way down to your abdomen. Breathe out, letting your stress flow

out with the air. Beginning with your feet and calves, slowly tense your muscles. Hold for several seconds, then release and relax the muscles. Slowly work your way through your major muscle groups using the same technique, until you have tensed and relaxed the muscles of your neck and face. Continue breathing deeply and enjoy the feeling of relaxation before opening your eyes.

Visualization. One of the most stressful aspects of a chronic disease such as arthritis is that it can make you feel as if your life is out of your control. Visualization helps reduce that stress by allowing you to imagine yourself anyway you like, doing anything you want to do. In other words, you are in control of the scenario. Also, by focusing on doing the things you like, you are not focusing on the things that cause you stress.

One form of visualization involves concentrating on pleasant scenes from your past or creating new situations in your mind. For example, you might try to remember every detail of a special holiday or of your first date with your spouse. Alternatively, you could imagine yourself taking your dream holiday or having a date with an attractive movie star.

Another form of visualization involves thinking of symbols that represent the pain or stress in different parts of your body. For example you might imagine that a painful knee or tense shoulder muscles are bright red, then imagine yourself making the red fade or change to cool, soothing blue. You might imagine your pain as a little monster that you could put in a rubbish bin and shut the lid or wrap in a small box that you drop into a post-box – with no return address, of course. For some specific mental exercises to help you relax, try the following techniques.

Sample Relaxation Exercises

For the following exercises, you'll never have to break a sweat or even leave your easy chair, because your mind is doing the work. The most important part of these exercises is that you be comfortable. Pick a place, get quiet and comfortable and start to focus on your breathing. Imagine that fresh air is coming in and tension is being released with every breath. Then try one or more of the exercises described below. Pick a favourite exercise to save for times when you're feeling stressed.

'Pain drain'. Feel within your body and note where you experience pain or tension. Imagine that the pain or tension is turning into a liquid substance. This heavy liquid flows down through your body and through your fingers and toes. Allow the pain to drain from your body in a steady flow. Now, imagine that a gentle stream flows down over your head . . . and further dissolves the pain . . . into a liquid that continues to drain away. Enjoy the sense of comfort and well-being that follows.

'Disappearing pain'. Notice any tension or pain that you are experiencing. Imagine that the pain takes the form of an object, or of several objects. It can be fruit, pebbles, crystals or anything else that comes to mind. Pick up each piece of pain, one at a time, and place it in a magic box.

As you drop each piece into the box, it dissolves into nothingness. Now, again survey your body to see if any pieces remain, and remove them. Imagine that your body is lighter now, and allow yourself to experience a feeling of comfort and well-being. Enjoy this feeling of tranquillity and repose.

'Healing potion'. Imagine you are in a chemist's that is stocked with bottles and jars of exotic potions. Each potion has a special magical quality. Some are of pure white light, others are lotions, balms and creams, and yet others contain healing vibrations. As you survey the many potions, choose one that appeals to you. It may even have your name on the container. Open the container and cover your body with that magical potion. As you apply it, let any pain or tension slowly melt away, leaving you with a feeling of comfort and well-being. Imagine that you place the container in a special spot and that it continually renews its contents for future use.

Biofeedback

Imagine being able to lower your heart rate or blood pressure or raise the temperature of your cold, achy hands at will. Using a process called biofeedback, the idea is not as far-fetched as it sounds. In fact, biofeedback can help you control many body processes that previously were considered to be out of conscious control. Biofeedback also can help you control your body's response to stress.

What is biofeedback? In a nutshell, it's the use of electronic instruments to measure body function and feed this back to you so that you can learn to control them. With practice, you can learn to control almost any body process that can be measured.

In a biofeedback session, sensors are attached to the part of the body being monitored – such as your cold hands or a stiff muscle in your neck – and then connected to an electronic instrument, such as computer. The instruments might read your skin temperature, electrical signals produced by your muscles, your heart rate or your brain waves.

The practitioner conducting biofeedback will teach you some relaxation techniques, such as visualization, to influence your subconscious body processes. As you practise these mental techniques, the instruments show with sound, light or other signals the effects that your thoughts are having on your body. Eventually, you will learn what mental relaxation techniques to use to get the physical effect you want, and you will be able to do them on your own without the equipment.

Keeping a Diary

When you were an adolescent, you may have found that confiding in a diary or journal – about a fight with your best friend, exam-time anxiety or a breakup with your latest sweetheart, for example – helped defuse some of the emotions that came with a stressful or hurtful experience. Research shows that a variation on the writing you may have done then can help you cope with the stress that comes with

arthritis now. Furthermore, a recent study of people with RA showed that those who regularly wrote about their most stressful life events experienced a 28 per cent reduction in overall disease activity.

Although it was just a single study, it substantiates long-held speculation that stress can contribute to disease activity. It also shows that reducing stress – specifically by writing about emotionally painful events – may decrease arthritis severity.

At the very least, keeping a journal can help you identify situations that cause you stress, and identifying stressors is the first step to finding ways to cope with or eliminate them. On page 145, you'll find a sample stress diary that you can use as a model to get you started. If you prefer a more free-form approach, try some of the following suggestions to begin your journaling:

- **Choose your pen and paper.** Find a spiral notebook or blank book with lots of open space to begin writing. Or, find a decorative notebook or journal at your local stationers or art supply shop. Select a pen or pencil with a comfortable grip that is easy to hold. If you prefer, write your journal on your computer.
- **Don't worry about penmanship or spelling.** A journal should be for your eyes only, so you won't need to impress anyone

with neat writing, proper grammar and expert spelling. Stopping to look up a word in the dictionary or to contemplate grammatical issues can interfere with self-expression.

- **Choose the time and place.** Don't try to write in your journal while you watch TV or stir a pot of soup on the stove. Pick a place without distractions and a time when you won't be interrupted. Focus entirely on your writing.
- **Don't hold back.** Don't be afraid to express your emotions – all of them. Your journal won't judge you and no one else will have to see it.
- **Pick your style.** You may wish to write about events as if you were a newspaper reporter covering your life, or you may wish to write your feelings in a letter – aren't there a few things you would like to tell arthritis? You may find one style that you'll want to stick with, or you may vary your style from day to day. It's your book – do what works for you.
- **Get help if you need it.** Writing can stir painful feelings, which themselves may be difficult to deal with – that's part of the process of letting go of pain and stress. If you feel you need help coping with the feelings that writing arouses, try talking to a counsellor. Sometimes taking your journal along with you to counselling – and reading selected passages aloud – can help your counsellor help you.

Arthritis Care publishes *Arthritis News*. It is a lifestyle magazine aimed at informing and entertaining, and giving people choices.

Complementary Therapies for Arthritis

12

CHAPTER 12:
COMPLEMENTARY THERAPIES FOR ARTHRITIS

While most of the treatments and therapies discussed in this book have been scientifically studied and prescribed or are used routinely by the medical profession, many of the therapies people with arthritis try and even swear by are not backed by scientific research. These therapies commonly are referred to as alternative or complementary therapies and include such treatments as herbs and nutritional supplements, magnets and copper bracelets.

Alternative and complementary therapies (also referred to as unproven remedies) are nothing new. In fact, many have their roots in ancient times. As people strive to take control of their own health care and to find natural alternatives to doctor-prescribed medications, the use of complementary and alternative therapies is increasing.

This growth may be especially noteworthy among people with painful, chronic diseases like arthritis for which there are no cures. If the medication your doctor prescribes isn't helping, you'd be tempted to try just about anything. And if you do try complementary therapy, the tendency of arthritis symptoms to come and go or wax and wane may make it seem like the therapy is working. Whether or not this is true may be hard to determine.

Let's say, for example, you put on a copper bracelet and the swelling goes down in your wrist. Was the copper bracelet responsible or would the swelling have gone down anyway? Or suppose you try a new nutritional supplement and discover that your joints are less painful and stiff. Did the nutritional supplement help or did your joints coincidentally get better?

Sometimes just the belief that a treatment will help is all it takes to bring some relief. Medical professionals refer to this as the *placebo effect* – a measurable effect on a person who has been given an inert substance or a fake therapy – and they suspect that it plays a big role in the effectiveness of many complementary therapies. The placebo effect may play a role in the seeming effectiveness of some complementary therapies in the relief of subjective symptoms like pain, fatigue or stiffness. In scientific studies of medications, the placebo effect is accounted for by not allowing patients (or the doctor administering the study) to know whether they are getting the medication studied.

Fortunately, as complementary therapies gain acceptance among patients and doctors, they also are being put to the test scientifically. A major aspect of the work by the Prince of Wales's Foundation for Integrated Health is to establish an evidence base, using a range of research and evaluation methods to identify safe and beneficial services. As doctors learn more about these therapies, the treatments may gain even wider acceptance.

In the meantime, if you want to try an unproven remedy, it's best to work closely with your doctor and to learn as much about the therapy as you can before you try it. At the same time, understand that there is not a lot of good scientific information about many complementary therapies, so you'll be proceeding at your own risk. Although many alternative therapies claim to be natural, even natural remedies aren't always safe. Many natural things – arsenic, uranium and poison ivy, to name a few – have obvious toxicities. Because they haven't been well studied, it is difficult to anticipate what side effects alternative therapies may have.

Be aware that such products as nutritional supplements may interact with your prescribed medications, either interfering with or adding to their action. Perhaps most dangerous, however, is the possibility that while using complementary remedies you may neglect the medical treatments your doctor prescribes – the ones that have proven benefits for people with arthritis. By all means use these remedies, once you have discussed them with your doctor, but treat them as complementary to the conventional remedies, not as alternatives.

In this chapter, we'll provide a brief overview of some of the most widely used or highly touted complementary and alternative therapies for arthritis. A more complete listing could easily fill a book. In fact, it has – *The Arthritis Foundation's Guide to Alternative*

Therapies has been published as a companion to this book. Of course, it is aimed at the US audience but readers can find many books on the subject of complementary therapies published in the UK. One that might be a good starting point is *The Which? Guide to Complementary Therapies by* Helen Barnet, published by the Consumers Association (which publishes *Which?* magazine). Arthritis Care's booklet *Balanced Approach* discusses complementary therapies and its *Food for Thought* has a section on supplements.

NUTRITIONAL SUPPLEMENTS

The most commonly used complementary therapies are nutritional supplements. These are vitamins, herbs, minerals and animal compounds purported to promote good health. Once sold only in nutrition or health-food stores, these products now line the shelves of almost every pharmacy, supermarket and discount store. Many are promoted and sold over the Internet and through multi-level marketing schemes.

High accessibility, ease of use and promises of being all-natural often make nutritional supplements popular among people seeking relief from arthritis pain and other symptoms. Do they work? And are they safe? Below is what we know about some of the supplements that commonly are used for arthritis and related conditions.

Glucosamine

Glucosamine is one of the hottest nutritional supplements for osteoarthritis –

and perhaps with good reason. Although it is not the cure for arthritis as some have claimed, it does seem to ease the pain and stiffness of osteoarthritis. In fact, there's a growing body of evidence that this supplement – which is extracted from crab, shrimp and lobster shells – may ease pain just as well as NSAIDs. There's even speculation that it may help repair damaged cartilage, but that claim has not been proved.

Research into glucosamine is being carried out in the UK and the USA, which should yield a better understanding of the supplement's role in treating OA. Since the supplement is safe for most people, if you can afford it, you may find it worthwhile to give it a try.

If you have diabetes, however, you may want to consult your doctor before taking glucosamine because it could potentially raise blood sugars.

Chondroitin Sulfate

In the body, naturally existing chondroitin sulfate is thought to draw fluid into the cartilage to help give it its elasticity and slow cartilage breakdown. The supplement, which is derived from cattle trachea, is often taken with glucosamine to ease the symptoms of osteoarthritis. Like glucosamine, chondroitin seems to be without serious side effects, so you may want to give it a try. But be prepared to wait for results. It can take two or more months for this supplement's effects to show.

Boswellia

Derived from a tree from Asia, boswellia (*Boswellia serrata*) comes in a standardized extract of the gum oleoresin. In animal and test tube studies, boswellia inhibits leukotriene synthesis, which contributes to inflammation. But studies have failed to consistently show any relief from pain and inflammation in people with arthritis.

The most common side effects of boswellia are diarrhoea, nausea or a rash. Otherwise, it is considered safe.

Cat's Claw

A vine that grows wild in the Peruvian Amazon, cat's claw (*Uncaria tomentosa*) gets its name from its claw-shaped thorns. The vine has a long tradition as a treatment for inflammation and 'bone pain'. At least one animal study shows that cat's claw just might prevent inflammation and other cell damage. However, there have been no human studies to document its effectiveness or its safety.

Cetyl Myristoleate (CMO)

Although you may see this advertised as a quick cure for many forms of arthritis, there is no accepted scientific evidence so far that CMO helps any form of arthritis – at least in people.

The claims for CMO stemmed from a 1993 study showing that injecting CMO into rats prevented them from developing arthritis. But one study on rats isn't reason enough to try a supplement that could be dangerous in people. Perhaps the most dangerous aspect of CMO is that some vendors advise people to stop taking methotrexate and corticosteroids first (saying that these drugs could interfere with CMO's action). By giving up your regular medications you could be sustaining irreparable joint damage as you wait to see if CMO might work. And you should *never* just stop taking corticosteroids.

DHEA/Prasterone

Short for dehydroepiandrosterone, DHEA is a mild male hormone produced naturally by the body. DHEA supplements have been touted as a cure for everything from cancer to old age. Most of its claims haven't been proved; the hormone is showing some promise as a therapy for lupus and is under review in the USA for approval as a prescription drug. Although it's not exactly clear how DHEA works for lupus, it is believed to restore an imbalance of male and female hormones in women with lupus.

Because DHEA carries the risk of side effects, ranging from acne to reduced levels of HDL (good cholesterol), you should only use it under the supervision of a doctor.

Dimethyl Sulfoxide (DMSO)

In the early 1960s, DMSO, a by-product of wood processing, was being hailed as a new therapy for all forms of arthritis. But studies of the substance were halted in the mid-'60s because high doses damaged the lens of the eye in animal studies. (No eye problems have been documented in human studies of DMSO.)

Today, DMSO is widely used in Russia and other countries for rheumatoid arthritis and osteoarthritis, but in the USA it has only one approved use – for a bladder condition called interstitial cystitis.

There is research that suggests DMSO can relieve pain and increase function for people with arthritis and that it may ease finger ulcers in scleroderma and relieve blood vessel constrictions in Raynaud's phenomenon. But the research is mixed. More studies are required to confirm DMSO's safety and effectiveness.

Echinacea

A North American wildflower, echinacea (*Echinacea purpurea, Echinacea angustifolia*) is one of the top-selling herbal products in the USA and Europe. The supplement has been touted as an immune system booster and as a treatment for a variety of ills, including the common cold.

Although echinacea has been widely studied, experts believe that much of the research is flawed. Although it could be useful against infections, experts say it could be harmful for people with autoimmune diseases, whose immune systems already may be overactive.

Kava Kava

A nonalcoholic drink from the root of the kava plant, kava kava has been shown to work

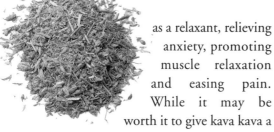

as a relaxant, relieving anxiety, promoting muscle relaxation and easing pain. While it may be worth it to give kava kava a try, doctors warn against mixing it with tranquillizers, antidepressants or alcohol, which could multiply the drink's effects.

Melatonin

A naturally occurring hormone that controls your sleep/wake cycle and helps regulate reproductive hormones, melatonin is made by the pineal gland deep in the brain, and our bodies make less of it as we age. In recent years, melatonin supplements have been touted as an immune system-booster and a sleep aid. Because fibromyalgia is associated with sleep difficulties, there has been speculation that melatonin might help, but research on its role in fibromyalgia has produced conflicting results. Experts advise against using it – particularly if you have an autoimmune disease, such as lupus, that could be made worse by boosting immune system activity.

MSM

Though touted on the Internet as one of the newest cures for arthritis, so far there is no scientific evidence to prove the effectiveness of MSM (short for methyl sulfonyl methane). MSM is a sulfur compound formed in the breakdown of DMSO. In animal studies, MSM has reduced arthritis symptoms. So far,

there have been no published human studies of MSM.

SAM-e/Ademetionine

S-adenosylmethionine, or SAM-e (pronounced 'sammy') for short, is a naturally occurring compound that is believed to improve joint mobility, relieve pain and ease depression. Although a number of European studies have shown that SAM-e relieves pain as effectively as several NSAIDs, in US studies SAM-e seemed to work for only mild pain.

Some studies have shown that SAM-e works as well as tricyclic antidepressants for depression – and with fewer side effects. One downside to SAM-e is its high cost. Any benefits last only as long as you take it.

HANDS-ON APPROACHES

Osteopathy

Until fairly recently, anyone could set themselves up as an osteopath. Now, however, an osteopath must have trained and reached a certain standard in order to practise. The organisation that regulates them is the General Osteopathic Council.

An underlying principle of osteopathy is the belief that problems with the musculoskeletal system can affect our health in many ways and that illness can, in turn, upset the balance of this system. Improved blood flow, through osteopathic manipulation – of the muscles around the joints and spine and sometimes of the bones and tissues of the skull and spine – can help restore balance and relieve ills.

Chiropractic

Once regarded as a 'quack' practice, chiropractic is now recognized as a legitimate method, with professionally qualified practitioners, and is growing in popularity. Used primarily for back or neck pain following an injury or accident, chiropractic is also sought for other problems, including joint pain and stiffness related to arthritis. Chiropractic focuses on manual adjustments and manipulation of the spine.

Although the origins of spinal manipulation probably go back to antiquity, chiropractic as we know it began in the 1890s and is based on the theory that misalignment of the vertebrae in the spine (called subluxation) is the cause of almost all diseases, and that chiropractic adjustment of the spine is the cure.

Some studies have suggested that chiropractic may help relieve pain from OA of the knee or from fibromyalgia. If you have joints that are inflamed, deformed or weakened by arthritis, use caution when considering chiropractic, because manipulating the fragile joints could cause irreparable damage.

Massage

Rather than a single therapy, massage actually refers to more than 100 types of body work, each with a different technique and philosophy. Although they have different approaches, they offer similar physical and emotional benefits for people with arthritis and related conditions. For more information on massage, see page 137.

THE BENEFITS OF COMPLEMENTARIES

If you feel frustrated about what medical science has to offer, complementary therapies – when used wisely – may offer benefits over what you're getting from the medication prescribed by your doctor. They may also give you the satisfaction that you are doing something for your disease. And some eventually may be scientifically proven to do what they claim. In fact, two supplements – glucosamine and chondroitin – are being studied in a major multicentre clinical trial.

If you decide to proceed with a complementary therapy – and many people with arthritis do – it's important to understand as much as you can about the therapy. (For more on making the decision about complementaries, see 'Evaluating Complementary Therapies' on page 159.) It's also important not to abandon any proven therapies that you need to keep your disease in check – or to lose hope in scientific-based medicine.

Though medical science seems to move slowly when you're coping with a chronic painful disease, advances are occurring more rapidly than ever before. In Chapter 13, we'll discuss the potential they may hold for you – and even how you can play a role in getting new drugs onto the market.

EVALUATING COMPLEMENTARY THERAPIES

When you're considering a complementary therapy, it pays to be cautious. In your search for relief you may be willing to try something that helps nothing but the wallet of the person selling it. Never assume a product is safe just because it's natural.

Follow this advice if you think you might like to try a complementary therapy:

- **Know the facts.** Although drugs and other conventional therapies are monitored and regulated by government agencies such as the Medicines and Healthcare products Regulatory Agency and the Committee on Dafety of Medicines, such therapies as herbs, supplements and some other alternatives do not have to undergo that type of scrutiny to be marketed.

- **Use good judgement.** If a practitioner makes unrealistic claims, such as, 'It will cure your arthritis', or suggests you discontinue your conventional treatments, consider it a strong warning that something is not right.

- **Seek out information.** Find out what training the practitioner has had and whether there is a professional organization that regulates the work and maintains standards.

- **Be a sceptic.** Beware of treatments that claim to work by a secret formula, say they are a cure or miraculous breakthrough, or are publicized in the backs of magazines, over the phone or through direct mail. Bona fide treatments are reported in medical journals.

- **Discuss it with your doctor.** Tell your doctor about any therapy you're trying, whether or not it is a complementary remedy. Your doctor can help you watch for and safeguard against side effects and possible negative interactions with medications you may be taking.

- **Consider the cost.** Some complementary therapies can be costly. If you have private health insurance, read your policy closely to find what therapies are covered and in what circumstances. Then compare your ultimate cost of a complementary therapy with that of a doctor-prescribed medication or treatment.

- **Proceed with caution.** If you decide to go through with a complementary treatment, seek out a qualified, licensed practitioner.

- **Don't abandon a treatment that works.** When starting a complementary therapy, don't stop taking the medication your doctor prescribes. Doing so could set you up for problems as diverse as heart problems or arthritis flares.

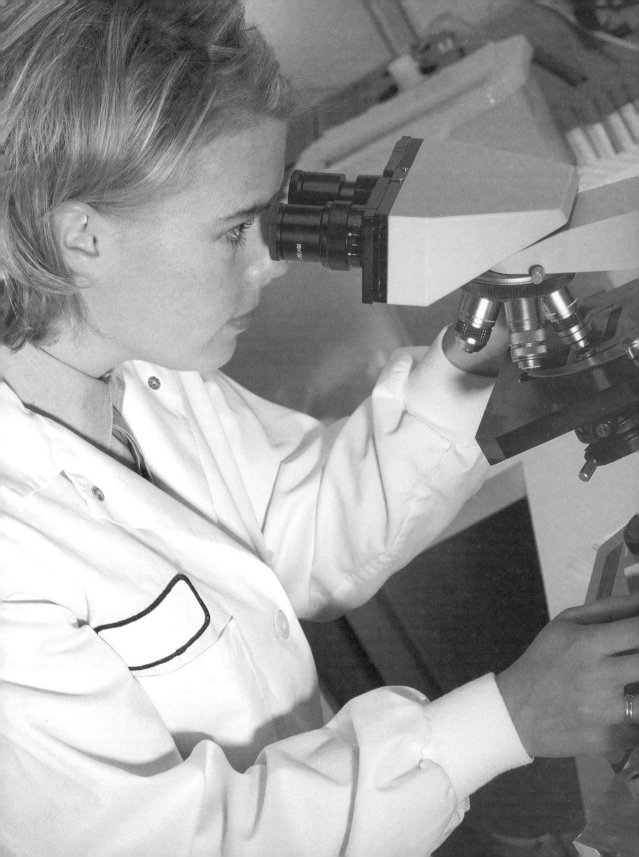

The Future of Arthritis

Arthritis

13°

CHAPTER 13:
THE FUTURE OF ARTHRITIS

In this age of quick fixes, it's hard to understand why someone doesn't just come up with the cure for arthritis. After all, medical science can cure many other conditions. A bacterial infection that once might have proven fatal may now be eradicated with a course of antibiotics. An inflamed appendix that might once have ruptured and killed a person can now be removed surgically with no long-term detrimental effects.

Whether arthritis will someday join these medical success stories, no one can say. Certainly, finding a cure is a goal of research scientists, yet arthritis is many diseases – more than 200 complex diseases. It's not possible that one medication will cure all of the forms of the disease – or even ease all symptoms. And it's highly unlikely that a single medication could ever cure a single form of the disease or work for all people with a particular form of the disease.

Furthermore, even if scientists found a way to stop arthritis permanently, the 'cure' would not undo any joint damage that has already taken place. That's why it's important to take advantage of all the good medications that are available today and to get proper treatment for your arthritis as soon as possible.

With today's medications, pain, joint deformity and organ damage are not inevitable consequences of arthritis-related diseases.

Powerful immunosuppressive drugs such as cyclophosphamide can relieve inflammation and prevent damage to the kidneys that can occur in people with systemic lupus erythematosus, and high-blood-pressure medications called angiotensin-converting enzyme (ACE) inhibitors can prevent kidney damage that once meant death or a lifetime of dialysis for people with the arthritis-related disease systemic sclerosis, or systemic scleroderma.

For people with rheumatoid arthritis and perhaps other inflammatory forms of the disease, disease-modifying antirheumatic drugs can do just what their name suggests – modify the course of the disease and delay or inhibit joint damage. Furthermore, three biological agents approved for rheumatoid arthritis – etanercept, infliximab and adalimumab – have been proven to delay or inhibit joint damage of rheumatoid arthritis.

UP-AND-COMING MEDICATIONS

In addition to all of the effective drugs that are available now, there are many others on the horizon that have caused great excitement. Some of them are still in early stages of clinical testing. Others may be approved in the near future.

Originally approved for cancer of the lymph nodes, rituximab is a monoclonal antibody that stops and destroys a type of white blood cell called B-lymphocytes. Because these lymphocytes are necessary to the production of rheumatoid factor and other self-directed antibodies in people with RA, UK researchers reasoned that wiping out these B-lymphocytes might also rid the body of these damaging antibodies.

A very preliminary and small trial suggests that those researchers may be on to something. In ten people treated with rituximab and then followed for 6 to 18 months, nine showed at least a 50 per cent improvement in their disease symptoms. Larger studies of the drug, which are to begin in the near future, should tell us more about the drug's potential in treating RA.

One of the greatest areas of advancement in rheumatoid arthritis treatment will probably come in the area of biological response modifiers. One biological agent, referred to as a recombinant human interleukin-1 receptor antagonist (IL-1ra) or by its generic and trade names (anakinra, *Kineret*), works by blocking the inflammatory cytokine IL-1ra.

These are just a few of the many medications in the works that have the potential to improve the health and lives of people with one of the 200-plus forms of arthritis and related conditions. Research is constantly going on to try to find better treatments, including drugs. But getting new drugs to market takes time. And for every drug in clinical testing that makes it, there are probably four more that don't pass the test. (For more on the drug-approval process, see 'How a Drug Makes It to Market' on page 168.)

STEM CELL TRANSPLANTATION

Despite the excitement of new medications, drugs are not the only new treatments on the horizon. One of the most exciting and promising treatments involves using existing immunosuppressive drugs in conjunction with autologous bone marrow or stem cell transplantation. Although the procedure is still highly experimental, it has been used with good results in some forms of arthritis.

The procedure involves removing so-called stem cells from a person's blood. Stem cells are 'mother cells' that have the capacity to expand and differentiate into many different types of cells, including infection-fighting T and B cells – the ones that go awry in some diseases.

After removing the stem cells, doctors administer high doses of immunosuppressive drugs to wipe out the patient's immune system. When existing immune cells are gone, the reserved stem cells are infused back into the patient, where, presumably, they will grow and differentiate into new immune system cells to replace the ones that were destroyed. So far, it appears that in some patients the new immune system created by their own stem cells does not malfunction the way the original immune system did.

In a recent study of seven women with lupus who had undergone stem cell transplants, all were relieved of signs of active lupus, and the functioning of their kidneys, hearts, lungs and immune systems – all of which had been affected by the disease – had returned to normal. Results in other diseases to date have not been as promising.

BEFORE YOU COMMIT TO A CLINICAL TRIAL

Before you sign up to participate in a study, it's essential to know what you're getting into. Here's how:

Speak to your doctor. Although your doctor may not be conducting the trial, he or she knows your medical condition more than any one else. Does he or she think this trial is a good idea? If so, why? If not, why not?

Read the fine print. Legally, the terms of participating in any study should be addressed in an informed consent form, which you'll be required to sign before you start. Don't hastily sign the form; ask to take it home and read over it carefully. You may even want to ask your spouse, a family member or a close friend to read it as well, in case you miss something.

Ask questions. If you still have questions after reading the informed consent form, don't hesitate to ask the doctor or other health-care professionals administering the study.

Here are some questions you might ask:

- What is the main purpose of the study?
- Are there any health risks involved?
- Do I have to stop taking my current medication(s)?
- What are the possible benefits?
- What happens if the study treatment harms me?
- Do I have the option of continuing the study treatment after the trial is over?
- Will I be paid to take part?

Although you should do your best to follow the doctor's instructions once you are in a trial (deviating from protocol could interfere with the accuracy of the study's results), you should never feel obliged to stay in a trial if you are uncomfortable about it. You have the right to leave the study at any time without it influencing your future medical care – regardless of what consent forms you have signed.

Despite such promising results in lupus, it's important to remember that the procedure is experimental, and it involves time, pain and risk. Between the time the original immune system is destroyed and when the new stem cells start to create a new one (about a month) the person would have to be hospitalized in a sterile room to avoid the risk of infection, because during that time – when, in effect, the person has no immune system – any infection could prove fatal.

Nevertheless, if your disease is active and severely affects your life, any promising procedure may be worth investigating. As yet, stem cell transplantation is available only to people enrolled in clinical studies and reserved for the most severe cases of disease which have not been helped by any other measures.

Even these therapies are just the tip of the iceberg. As scientists learn more about the genetics of the different forms of arthritis, other factors that contribute to the diseases and individuals' responses to those factors, new treatments will emerge and doctors will be able to apply them early with increasingly better control. At any time there may be as many as a dozen or more new treatments in late stages of clinical testing for arthritis-related diseases. Each has the potential to be an improvement in some way over the drugs we have now, for at least some people.

YOU CAN PLAY A ROLE IN RESEARCH

What you might not know is that, as a person with arthritis, you have an opportunity to play a role in the development of and testing of new treatments. Each year, thousands of people do, by enrolling in what are called clinical trials. A clinical trial is a carefully designed study of a potential new drug, medical treatment or medical device on a group of people with a particular condition. These studies, which are required for a treatment to be approved for use, are typically funded by the manufacturer of the drug or device being tested. Without people like you, there could be no studies – and thus no new arthritis treatments.

Taking part in a clinical trial offers several potential benefits both to you and to others in similar situations. First, taking part in a trial may allow you to receive cutting-edge med-

ications and treatments before anyone else does, free of charge. During the course of the study, you will probably be followed up more frequently and monitored more closely than would be usual for standard treatment. Some clinical trials may also pay a fee to cover expenses. Some may even pay more than that.

Even if a study doesn't benefit you personally, your contribution to it will help add to knowledge of arthritis and perhaps help improve the lives of others with the disease.

As with any treatment – in fact, anything in life – there are also some potential drawbacks to participating in a trial. For one, you may not receive the new treatment being tested. In every clinical trial, a new treatment is compared to an existing treatment and/or a placebo (a 'sham' procedure or pill without active ingredients).

That means you have chance – usually as high as 50/50 – of being in the other group. Also, because you may be receiving a new treatment that hasn't been used widely or for long, there is no way of knowing, with certainty, what the long-term effects of treatment might be. Furthermore, taking part in a trial for one drug may require that you stop taking a drug that has been helpful to you. For all of those reasons, most doctors should advise against taking part in a clinical trial if you are doing well with the medication you are taking.

Even if you choose not to take your chances with a new medical treatment, there are still ways you can contribute to research. One opportunity is by taking part in genetic

Identifying Good Research

When it comes to reports about arthritis research, how can you separate the good from the bad or useless? A good starting point is to evaluate all you read by using the following criteria:

Consider the source:

Was it published in a peer-reviewed journal? The most reliable studies are those published in reputable journals and that have been reviewed by other doctors in the field prior to publication. Vague references to being scientifically tested may mean nothing.

Who did the research?

Was the person conducting the research from an institution you have heard of? Does the article say who funded the study? Research funded by the Arthritis Research Campaign or the National Institutes of Health, for example, is usually reliable.

Who was studied?

While the research may be good, it may mean nothing for you if the people in the study were in a different situation from yours. In other words, a new drug that looks promising in treating 100 women with rheumatoid arthritis may be of no use for a man who has osteoarthritis.

Have you seen similar reports elsewhere?

When evaluating a report in a magazine or newspaper or on a web site, check around and see if you find similar information elsewhere. When writing about technical medical information, it's easy for a writer to get facts wrong. If you see consistent reports in several locations, however, it's more likely to be correct.

registries. This is a process in which a researcher takes a blood sample and then compares your genes to those of people with and without the disease to look for similar and dissimilar genetic factors.

Another way to help arthritis research is by taking part in epidemiological studies, in which a researcher may ask you questions about diet, exercise and other lifestyle factors, for example, that may play a role in a certain form of arthritis. Some studies involve filling out questionnaires from time to time.

If you think you might like to participate in a clinical trial, consult your doctors. They might be aware of a trial for which you would be a candidate. In fact, they may be involved in such a trial themselves.

Much of the clinical research that leads to the approval of new arthritis medications is conducted by rheumatologists, both in major medical centres and independent practices. Sometimes you can learn about clinical trials through advertisements on local radio stations or in the newspaper but this is uncommon.

The Arthritis Research Campaign web site has a section of news, which includes information about forthcoming studies and research. An example is a study to see if vitamin D supplements will help with the pain of osteoarthritis in the knees.

KEEPING UP WITH RESEARCH

Whether or not you take part in medical research, you'll certainly want to know the results of research that is taking place.

Getting the news isn't really that difficult – just open the newspaper, turn on the radio or TV, surf the Internet or ask your doctor. As more people have arthritis and as researchers learn more about it and develop new drugs to treat it, arthritis is a frequent topic discussed in the media. For example, a query was raised as to whether using a Blackberry handheld can contribute to someone getting repetitive strain injury (RSI), which, like carpal tunnel syndrome, is a form of arthritis. There is no evidence specifically related to Blackberry but the over-use of handheld devices is linked to RSI.

What is more difficult is finding news that is accurate and putting it into context. It's important that you get your information from reliable sources, such as updates on medical research published in *Arthritis News*, and scrutinize what you read.

For tips on evaluating the research information you read, see 'Identifying Good Research' on page 166.

THE PROGNOSIS FOR LIFE WITH ARTHRITIS

Although no two people and no two cases of arthritis are exactly alike, the odds are that you will live a fulfilling, productive and long life – if you choose to.

While life with a chronic disease holds no certainties, a lot of what happens to you is up to you. Will you take your medications as prescribed? Will you consult your doctor about potential drug reactions or other potential problems? Will you make commitment to exercise and eat healthily, even when it would be a lot easier not to? Will you take advantage of some of the non-medication techniques that are available to get you through painful times? Will you take an active role in your own health care?

And finally, perhaps the hardest question of all: Will you keep a positive attitude even on days when you feel you have nothing to feel positive about?

Studies show that attitude is an important part of managing arthritis. People who do well tend to recognize the positive aspects of their lives rather than the negatives ones. If you

HOW A DRUG MAKES IT TO MARKET

Despite great advances in medical care, many chronic disease still exists, and the pharmaceutical industry constantly seeks innovative new medications to combat them. Of course, the protection of patients from harm is paramount where medications are concerned, and a number of steps are taken in their development specifically to ensure that as much is known about the safety and efficacy of new medications as is possible to determine before they are available for wider use to patients.

New medicines are discovered by a number of routes. Many years ago new compounds reached patients largely by serendipity, now with increasing knowledge about the nature of many chronic diseases scientists are increasingly targeting specific disease processes with increasing success. The hope is that by matching new drugs much more closely to a disease target, many more damaging side effects might be avoided.

Medications in development are screened for potential problems as well as benefits via a number of methods, including computer modelling of effects, test-tube experiments to test theories about disease modification, and eventually animal

experiments to determine as much as possible about safety and effectiveness. Animal experiments provide crucial information about potential new drugs, but during the past few years the number of animal experiments has stayed roughly the same although research activity has mushroomed.

Once the 'pre-clinical' testing is complete, a file of results is reviewed by both the European licensing body for new medicines (the EMEA) and an independent ethics committee before tests in people can commence. When safety criteria have been satisfied, Phase 1 studies can begin.

Phase 1 studies take place in very small numbers of volunteers. They are used to determine the best way to give a new medicine (e.g. injection, tablet or patch), how quickly it breaks down once it is given, whether the medicine or any breakdown products might cause harm, and some early information about potential positive effects.

Phase 2 studies take place in patients, usually up to 100–200. These studies are used to determine the most effective dose of a drug, and to expand our safety knowledge. Surrogate markers to tell us about long-term effects might be used; for example, changes in substances that cause inflammation might be a long-term sign of positive effects on arthritis or other inflammatory conditions.

Phase 3 studies take place in hundreds of patients, out in a real world setting such as a GP clinic or local hospital. They are designed to replicate as much as possible 'real-life' conditions where a new medicine would be used. The new medicine is compared against the best possible alternative or an inactive compound – a 'placebo'. Trials take place over a period of six months or more so that effectiveness and safety can be measured much more accurately.

Once Phase 3 studies are complete, a licence can be applied for to make a new treatment available to doctors for their patients. In Europe that new licence comes from the EMEA only once a study report has been reviewed by expert scientists from a number of different countries.

Once a new medicine is launched, the responsibilities of the pharmaceutical company and the regulator, the Committee on Safety of Medicines, continue. Almost all companies now conduct **Phase 4** studies into their products to demonstrate longer-term safety, efficacy and value for money. The regulator and pharmaceutical companies keep new medicines under intensive surveillance, watching for any early signal of problems, specifically for the protection of patients.

For more information on the development of new medicines and the British pharmaceutical industry as a whole, visit the ABPI web site (www.abpi.co.uk).

Information kindly provided by
Dr Phil Amery, MBChB, MRCP, MFPM,
of GlaxoSmithKline UK

really think about it, you will probably realize that there are a lot of positives in your own life.

Arthritis may change your life, but it does not have to control it. While it would be dangerous to deny that you have arthritis and neglect your treatment, it may be as harmful in other ways to make arthritis and its treatment the entire focus of your life.

After all, you are still you. If arthritis makes it difficult to do the things you used to do, look for new ways to do them. Or, look for similar activities you can enjoy.

For instance, if you can't go hill walking, perhaps you can enjoy the scenery from the top of a hill reached by car or enjoy a less strenuous walk through the countryside. If arthritis cuts short a football career, maybe you could pursue a career in coaching or volunteer at your local sports centre. If arthritis in your hands makes it difficult to whip up a gourmet meal from scratch, you can still prepare delicious and nutritious dinners with fresh, pre-cut or frozen vegetables and some help from your local supermarket's deli.

Although having arthritis will never be easy, the prognosis is getting better all the time, with new treatments and new approaches to self-management. With expanding technology as well as the vast array of low-tech things you can do for yourself, you can live a long, fulfilling life despite arthritis. But it's largely up to you.

We hope that *Managing Your Arthritis* has been an informative resource for you as you learn more about arthritis, its treatment and self-management. Let this book serve as a springboard to learning more about your disease and to incorporating self-management techniques into your daily living. In the UK, Arthritis Care also offers many other resources for educating yourself about arthritis and related conditions, and ways to get involved with your local arthritis community.

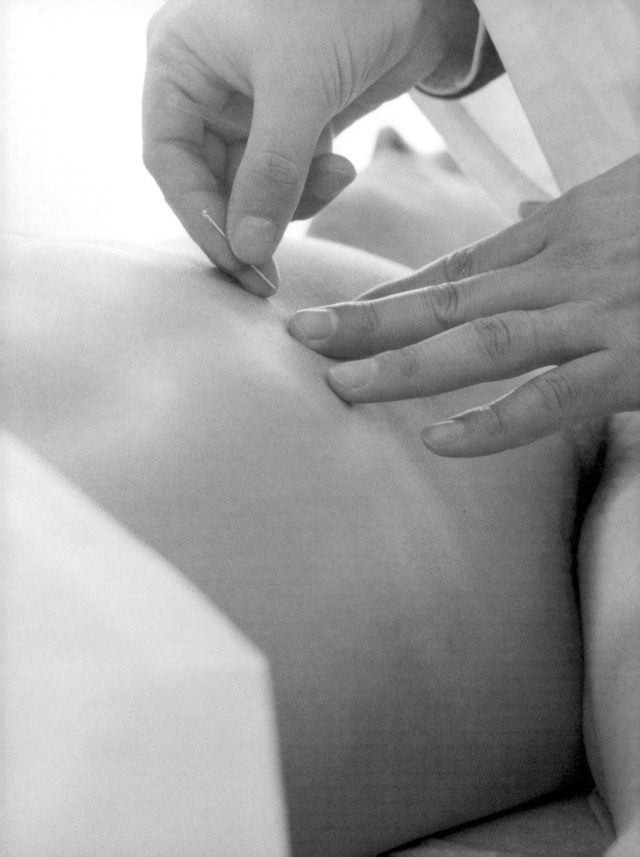

Review of Massage, Manipulation and Other Therapies

14

CHAPTER 14: REVIEW OF MASSAGE, MANIPULATION AND OTHER THERAPIES

Most complementary therapies for pain relief don't involve taking herbs or nutritional supplements. There are many other philosophies of healing, as well as treatments performed by practitioners of these philosophies, that are increasing in popularity for people with chronic pain.

Some of these treatments rise from ancient healing traditions in China or India. Others stem from relatively recent health philosophies. No matter how old or new these complementary treatments are, they tend to spark controversy, as well as debate among doctors and their patients.

No matter what therapy you try, it's important to find out if the practitioner is a member of the relevant professional society (see the Resources section) and has the proper training to perform the procedures. Never allow a practitioner who is not properly licensed to perform any type of manipulation or treatment on your body. You should agree on fees and terms beforehand so you will know what charges you will owe for these services.

Consult your GP also so he knows what therapies you are exploring. In some cases, your doctor can refer you to reputable, qualified practitioners of various therapies. Some doctors also perform these therapies as part of their integrative practice. In addition, some physiotherapists, occupational therapists or other health-care professionals may offer some of these services.

ACUPUNCTURE AND ACUPRESSURE

Acupuncture is an ancient, Asian healing technique that has gained popularity in the West over the past few decades. Mainstream medical institutions now take acupuncture seriously and are studying the therapy to determine why and how well it works. Many UK national charities and research organizations have funded research on acupuncture to explore its effectiveness.

Acupuncture is part of *Chinese medicine.* Chinese medicine, which may also involve herbs, massage, meditation techniques or exercises, developed over thousands of years in China, but has gained new popularity in the West in recent years. One of the main reasons people seek acupuncture treatment is to relieve chronic pain, especially back pain, arthritis or fibromyalgia. Currently, a number of scientific studies are being conducted to research the effectiveness and safety of acupuncture treatment specifically for osteoarthritis and other diseases involving chronic pain.

Acupuncture involves a trained professional puncturing the skin with very thin needles at any of 300 specific sites on the body. These points lie along energy pathways called *meridians*. Devotees of acupuncture believe that the placement of needles at these points will increase the energy flow (called qi; pronounced *chee*) along the meridians. Qi is, in traditional Chinese belief, essential to healthy balance in the body, known as yin and yang. *Acupressure* is another form of this treatment, but one involving hand pressure rather than needle punctures.

Acupuncture supposedly boosts the body's natural ability to heal itself and relieve pain.

Studies about acupuncture have found some merit to these claims. They find that some people have higher levels of endorphins, those natural pain-fighting chemicals the body produces, in their cerebrospinal fluid after acupuncture.

Scientists do not yet understand why pricking the skin at these particular points causes the endorphin boost, or why acupuncturists place their needles in one part of the body to get pain relief in another part. Acupuncture may stimulate the flow of electromagnetic signals through the body along the meridians, helping endorphins flow. Acupuncture may also activate the release of the central nervous system's natural opiates (similar to the chemicals in opiate drugs), which relieve pain. Or it may aid in the release of certain neurotransmitters, body chemicals that play a role in how the brain relays pain messages, and *neurohormones*, brain chemicals that can affect the function of the body's organs.

More scientific studies are necessary if acupuncture is to be established as a pain-relief treatment, but the procedure may well provide relief from many painful conditions, including headache, tennis elbow, fibromyalgia, myofascial pain, osteoarthritis, low back pain, carpal tunnel syndrome and more. Most doctors who support the use of acupuncture believe it should be used as a complement to regular medical treatment of chronic pain. Many countries have licensing boards that license acupuncturists and other individuals who practise 'healing arts' to perform treatments. In the UK, consult the British Acupuncture Council (see the Resources section for their details).

What Happens During Acupuncture? During an acupuncture session, the practitioner (known as an acupuncturist) will take a medical history and examine you (particularly your pulses and your tongue) to help him make a traditional Chinese medicine diagnosis. He will then select a number of points on your body to use in your treatment. Using a new sterile needle each time, the acupuncturist will insert the needles and leave them there while you lie on a table for about 20 minutes. He may rotate the needles during this time – a practice thought to achieve greater effect. (In acupressure, he applies pressure, not needles, to these points.) Some acupuncturists also use electrical stimulation of the needles to boost the procedure's effects, a procedure known as *electroacupuncture*. Others use dried herbs as part of their treatment of the patient, a practice called *moxibustion*.

The acupuncturist will then remove the needles and will probably ask you to rest some more before rising from the table. Reactions to the procedure vary widely from person to person. You may feel light-headed or drowsy, so you should not drive yourself home from your first session. Usually, repeated treatments are needed for relief of chronic pain.

To find an acupuncturist in your area, first ask your doctor for a referral. If he cannot give you any information, consult the British Acupuncture Council, the national body that certifies acupuncturists. (See the Resources section for contact details.)

Acupressure. Acupressure is a massage-like technique where the practitioner presses on particular points of the body in an attempt to relieve pain that may occur in other areas of the body. According to the theory behind the therapy, these acupoints occur on energy pathways, or meridians, as in acupuncture, and the therapy is designed to restore proper energy flow and balance to relieve pain.

MANIPULATION THERAPIES

One popular treatment for pain relief, particularly of chronic neck and back pain or post-injury pain, is *manipulation therapy*, or manual adjustment of the spine or the limbs in order to restore proper alignment or promote the body's natural healing ability. Many different health-care professionals perform manipulation therapy, and the therapy they offer may vary slightly from discipline to discipline. Chiropractors are probably the most common practitioners of this therapy, but osteopaths, physiotherapists and even some doctors may also perform it.

Chiropractic and Osteopathy

Chiropractic is a system that holds that pain and many other health problems, including minor and serious diseases, occur because the body's spine is out of alignment. Chiropractors perform regular adjustments to the spine, or *spinal manipulations,* in order to restore the spine to its optimal position. According to the philosophy of chiropractic, a well-adjusted spine allows the body to perform its natural defences of pain and disease at optimal levels.

Whilst there is dispute among scientists as to the validity of the theory of chiropractic, many people seek chiropractors and other health-care professionals for periodic or regular spinal manipulation as a therapy for pain. Whether or not the therapy works, or whether or not the overall philosophy behind it is valid, is a matter of opinion at this point.

Chiropractic began in 1895 in Iowa, when a lay healer named David Daniel Palmer formed the basic theory of what was then called vertebral subluxations. His treatment philosophy spread.

In the UK, chiropractors are registered with the General Chiropractic Council, the statutory body for regulating the profession. Over 50 per cent of chiropractors are represented by the British Chiropractic Association (BCA); they will have undergone a four-year full-time internationally accredited degree course. Chiropractors cannot prescribe drugs or perform surgery, but they do consult with patients and perform manipulation and other treatments.

Osteopathy was founded in the 19th century, by a US Civil War surgeon named Andrew Still, who was disillusioned by the failures of the mainstream medicine of his time. He devised his own theory that the body's musculoskeletal system was key to good health and the body's ability to defend itself against disease and to heal itself following injury.

Osteopathy uses many of the same practices and follows many of the same principles as traditional or allopathic medicine. In the examination room, osteopathic treatment may be quite similar to examinations by a doctor. However, osteopaths may focus more on general health and wellness practices, as well as addressing the home and work environment of the patient.

As osteopathic medicine is based on the idea that the musculoskeletal system is at the root of many diseases and pain conditions, osteopaths receive additional training in treating the musculoskeletal system. Their treatment may include *osteopathic manipulative treatment,* using their hands on the body of the patient in an effort to diagnose disease, damage to tissues and more. Treatment may also include manipulation, where the osteopath uses his hands more forcefully to correct problems in the musculoskeletal system.

What Happens During Manipulation Therapy? Manipulation therapy usually follows a consultation with the practitioner. He may determine your range of motion (the amount of flexibility you have in certain joints), muscle tone or strength, reflexes and more. Then, the practitioner might perform the manipulation therapy, along with prescribing treatments and suggestions, such as exercise or dietary changes.

Spinal manipulation involves the practitioner using either his hands or a small pushing instrument to press on the spine, back and neck or, sometimes, the limbs. The manipulation often looks as if they are pushing or stretching your neck and back into alignment, while you lie on your stomach on a padded table. You may hear a crack or pop, but this is simply air being released from the moving vertebrae. The practitioner may get you to rest for a few moments after the manipulation.

Study results and professional opinions are mixed on the benefit of spinal manipulation therapy for people with chronic pain. You may have to rely on your own judgement as to whether this therapy is worth trying. If you try spinal manipulation therapy and do not see some relief after three or four sessions, it probably isn't going to work. You may receive some pain relief from the manipulations, but if you don't see improvement, try massage, water therapy, exercise or other techniques instead.

Be wary of any practitioner who claims that continual manipulations throughout your lifetime are necessary to achieving pain relief and good health; there is no evidence to support this claim. Also, be wary of any practitioner who suggests that you discontinue any other medical treatment or seeing your medical doctors for care.

Although it's likely that spinal manipulation is safe, people with inflammatory arthritis or osteoporosis should use caution because manipulation might damage weakened joints or bones. Fracture of bones can occur. It's essential to inform your chiropractor, osteopath, physiotherapist or any other spinal manipulation practitioner about your health conditions. Don't just say, 'I'm in pain.' Practitioners need to know any possible health problems you may have in order to perform manipulation properly. If manipulation causes pain, stop the treatment and inform the practitioner.

Your doctor should be able to refer you to a qualified practitioner of manipulation therapy in your area. Chiropractors and osteopaths are required by law to be registered with the relevant regulatory body: the General Chiropractic Council and the General Osteopathic Council Association.

Craniosacral Therapy

A similar form of manipulation therapy, although one less widely practised, is *craniosacral therapy*. This therapy aims to balance the fluids in what practitioners term the craniosacral system – the fluids that run down your spinal cord from the brain to the base of the spine. Practitioners and devotees believe an imbalance in this fluid can cause various health problems, including pain.

In craniosacral therapy, the practitioner stands behind you while you lie on a comfortable table, and gently holds your head in his hands while applying soft pressure to various

points on the back of the neck. He may also apply gentle pressure to points at the base of the spine. Experts are very divided on the validity or usefulness of this procedure. Some people find it beneficial or relaxing.

Some chiropractors and osteopaths perform *cranial manipulation*, in which they apply gentle pressure to the skull in certain areas in order to relieve pain. They use the heels of their hands and press on particular points of the skull. Some professionals use this technique to relieve chronic neck and back pain, ear pain, and even *tinnitus* (a chronic ringing or buzzing in the ears). Some of these practitioners believe that the cranial manipulation doesn't relieve the pain, but corrects misalignment of the skull's bones (which actually don't move) so the body's natural defence system can work more effectively.

MASSAGE

Massage is a common procedure used by many people who are not in chronic pain but enjoy the soothing action of massage for stress relief or improvement in flexibility. But many people use massage for pain relief, and studies show that this is an effective, safe therapy when administered by a qualified professional. Massage therapists are plentiful and located in almost every area, and their fees should be affordable.

'Massage' is a common term and there are several different types of massage. In a nutshell, massage is the manual manipulation and kneading of soft tissues, particularly muscles. Massage's benefits include improved blood circulation, relaxation of tense muscles, improved range of motion and increased endorphin levels – all of which may benefit people with chronic pain. Massage may enable you to feel more flexible and relaxed, so you sleep better and are more able to exercise regularly to maintain good health.

Below is a rundown of the different types of massage therapy. Ask your doctor or physiotherapist to suggest what type of massage is appropriate for your type of pain.

Swedish massage. This is the most common form of massage, and the form most people think of when they hear 'massage'. Swedish massage therapists knead the top layers of muscles of the body, often applying lotion or oil to ease their hand movements. Swedish massage usually lasts between 30 minutes and an hour. Some sessions are relaxing and others involve harder, more vigorous pressing designed to loosen tense muscles.

Deep tissue massage. This type of massage therapy involves a deeper, harder pressing by the therapist in order to release tension in the deepest layers of soft tissue. Therapists might use their fingers, elbows or thumbs to press between layers of muscles and get to the sources of pain or tension. Some people may experience soreness after the first few sessions, but later may find relief of nagging pain, such as low back pain or arthritis.

Trigger point therapy or neuromuscular massage. Trigger points are painful or tense points in the body that may be triggering pain elsewhere. In order to release the muscle tension that may be causing pain, practitioners use their fingers to press deeply into the body and massage those points. Some people with fibromyalgia find this therapy useful for temporary pain relief, but it can be a painful experience for others.

Myofascial release massage. Myofascial pain is centred in the fascia – the fibrous, thin connective tissues beneath the skin, sheathing your muscles. In this massage therapy, practitioners gently massage and stretch the fascia in order to release tension in these structures. Typically, myofascial release therapy sessions last about 30 minutes, and don't use oil as in Swedish massage. People with myofascial pain, as well as fibromyalgia and pain caused by tension or stress, may find relief with this therapy.

Oriental massage techniques. Many Oriental medicine practitioners perform techniques designed to restore the flow of qi in the body. *Shiatsu* massage is a Japanese technique that is gaining popularity in the West and is widely available at spas and health clubs where massage is offered. It's similar to acupressure because it aims to improve the flow of energy along the meridians. Sessions may take place on a table or a mat on the floor, and include stretching techniques as well.

A less widely practised Oriental massage technique is *tuina,* a Chinese therapy that includes massaging the body's pressure points.

Rolfing. Rolfing (named for its inventor, Ida Rolf) involves a technique very similar to deep tissue massage, and the idea is that tightness in the fascia may be causing pain. Rolfing aims to release muscles and other soft tissues from the fascia so that the body can restore its natural healing ability, aiming more at body maintenance than treating disease. Usually, Rolfing therapy takes place in ten one-hour sessions held about a week apart.

Hellerwork is a similar, massage-based practice that also involves exercises and teaching the person better posture and movement techniques in order to prevent pain.

Skinrolling technique. Some people with fibromyalgia find pain relief from this type of massage. Skinrolling involves a therapist picking up a roll of the person's skin and moving it carefully back and forth across the fascia, the fibrous tissues underneath. This technique aims to break the connections between the tissue and the nerve endings under them that are communicating the pain messages. Skinrolling can be painful at first, so therapists may use a mild anaesthetic before the treatment. Some people have reported long-lasting relief from fibromyalgia pain after skinrolling, but others find the technique itself too painful.

Spray and stretch technique. This kind of massage is used by people with fibromyalgia and also by people experiencing chronic back pain. Experts are divided as to its validity. Spray and stretch is usually performed by a physiotherapist rather than a massage therapist. The doctor or therapist sprays the skin over the painful area with a cooling anaesthetic, such as ethyl chloride, and then gently kneads the tense, painful muscles.

With any type of massage therapy, you should feel some relief after the session or at least in a few days. Most people who rely on massage therapy for pain relief schedule appointments regularly, as often as their doctor or physiotherapist might suggest.

To find a qualified therapist, ask your doctor for a referral, or consult a physiotherapy clinic or pain clinic in your area. If you use the services of a spa, make sure you check the credentials of the practitioners – they should be trained professionals. Be wary of so-called 'massage parlours' or 'health spas', which may offer cheaply priced massages performed by untrained people.

You can also perform your own massage to certain areas of the body that may be painful, such as wrists, arms, legs, feet, neck or shoulders. It may be difficult for you to reach your own back, but you may be able to massage your own lower back. Massage devices are available at many shops. These devices can help you massage sore joints or muscles, and some can apply soothing heat as well.

Reflexology

Somewhat similar to massage but more focused on a specific area of the body, *reflexology* is a pain-relief technique that is more akin to acupressure than traditional Swedish, full-body massage.

Reflexology practitioners believe that the hands, feet and ears have particular pressure points that correlate to different areas of the body or organs. When they apply pressure to these points, the correlating body part that is painful will experience pain relief. For example, pressing on the heel might aid pain in the sciatic nerve, which is located in the back. Whether or not this theory is valid – and there are few studies to suggest that it is – some people find the treatment soothing and relaxing. This may be due to the placebo effect because they believe that the treatment will ease their pain.

OTHER PAIN-RELIEF THERAPIES

There are numerous pain-relief therapies that either fall outside the standard medical treatment spectrum or are somewhat experimental. Many of these therapies are performed or prescribed by doctors and other mainstream health-care professionals, such as physiotherapists. Before trying any of these therapies, talk to your doctor and, if you have private health insurance, check the policy for coverage.

TENS

Earlier in the book, we discussed implants that release electrical stimulation of nerves in order to relieve pain. Another type of electricity-based therapy is TENS, or transcutaneous electrical nerve stimulation. TENS uses electrical stimulation to the nerves to block pain signals from getting to the brain. Many doctors now suggest that their patients try this pain treatment, especially people with back pain, arthritis, fibromyalgia or nerve-related pain. You can administer TENS yourself.

TENS is not painful and requires no needles, surgery or drugs, so it's gaining in popularity as a treatment for chronic pain. Usually, TENS helps people with pain concentrated in a particular area of the body, rather than all-over pain.

What Happens During TENS? Your doctor or another practitioner will place small electrodes on your skin in the area where you are experiencing pain. The electrodes are connected to a small, battery-operated box that releases low-level electricity. When the box passes a current, you feel a tingling sensation. If successful, TENS provides temporary pain relief.

TENS machines cost about £50. They can be used by almost anyone, although people with widespread pain may not be able to use TENS. For some people, it offers short-term pain relief when other treatments fail to do so.

Ask your doctor about TENS. If there is a pain clinic in your area, the facility may be able to lend or hire you a TENS machine. Tell your doctor if you decide to try TENS, to make sure you are a good candidate.

Biofeedback

As we learned in Chapter 1, the brain is the control centre for all pain messages. The way your cerebral cortex perceives the pain messages, sent via the peripheral nerves and the spinal cord, can depend on many things. Can the brain learn to control the way it senses pain, perhaps reducing the intensity of the pain? A treatment called *biofeedback* is based on the belief that it can.

Biofeedback is a treatment technique in which you are trained to reduce your pain by using signals from your own body. A machine picks up electrical signals in the muscles (electromyographs or EMGs). These are translated into a form you can detect: the machine triggers a flashing light bulb, perhaps, or activates a beeper every time there is an increase in your muscle activity.

When you experience pain, you may tense your muscles, which in turn may produce more pain. If you are made aware of this increased muscle activity using an EMG feedback machine, you can then use a variety of techniques to relax your muscles, all the time getting feedback via your EMG on how successful you are being. The biofeedback machine acts as a kind of sixth sense which allows you to 'see' or 'hear' activity inside your body.

This treatment is recommended for people with fibromyalgia, but is less successful in people with arthritis.

What happens during biofeedback? In biofeedback, the doctor or therapist attaches electrodes or sensors to various parts of your body, particularly areas where you might be feeling pain or tension. The electrodes are connected to a computer or other instruments that record the various reactions you have to pain: body temperature, heart rate, muscle tension or even brain waves.

Then, you'll learn some mind-control techniques, such as visualization (focusing on pleasant imagery or fantasies where you are in control of your pain), or relaxation techniques, such as deep breathing. The biofeedback equipment should be able to show you how your relaxation techniques are affecting your body's processes. The practitioner will teach you to use these techniques to control your muscles and, therefore, your heart rate and blood flow. You'll have to do this several times and practise the techniques on your own. Eventually, you should be able to do these techniques on your own and see a positive result.

Does biofeedback really work? Some research shows that it can work, and learning relaxation therapies and seeing how they can affect your pain response is a positive, risk-free treatment option. You are learning to take control of your own body and your own reaction to pain. There is evidence that biofeedback can help relieve many forms of chronic pain, such as back pain, and tension and migraine headaches.

Hydrotherapy, Water Exercise and Balneotherapy

Better known as soaking in a hot tub, Jacuzzi™ or pool spa, *hydrotherapy* seems like a natural way to massage painful muscles and joints, or to relax the body in order to reduce painful muscle tension. You can explore hydrotherapy on your own, such as in your bathtub, hot tub or home whirlpool bath; at a health spa (in fact the word 'spa' is an acronym for the Latin term *sante per aqua*, or 'health by water'); or under medical supervision at a pain clinic or rehabilitation centre.

The soothing but gentle pressure of water jets against sore, tightened or tense muscles can relieve back pain and other muscle-related pain. People with chronic pain syndromes that involve stress can find the soaking and bubbling action of the warm water relaxing. And soaking in warm or hot water is a widely recommended therapy for people with the joint pain and stiffness of arthritis. So hydrotherapy is an easy, low-risk therapy for many people in pain, something that may not completely relieve their pain but can be added as a complementary therapy to their pain-management plan. Hydrotherapy provides only temporary relief from chronic pain.

Some people cannot use hot tubs or spas, depending on their health condition. People with high blood pressure or diabetes or those taking some medicines should avoid hot tubs for health reasons. Ask your doctor if this therapy is appropriate for you and what, if any, precautions you should take. Do not mix alcohol or sedative drugs with hydrotherapy, as you could become drowsy and fall asleep in the water.

Another type of hydrotherapy is water exercise, or aquarobics, a highly recommended and widely available therapy that is easy for most people with chronic pain to do. Exercises performed in warm pools allow the person to increase flexibility, cardiovascular health and muscle strength without the pain and strain of traditional land exercise. Tell the leader about your condition so that you do not over-exercise and then feel worse when you get out of the pool.

A similar therapy that may provide warmth and relief to sore body parts is *balneotherapy*, or mud therapy. You may be familiar with mudpacks or herbal body wrap treatments at fancy spas as a way to relax the spirit. Some people also use warm mud compresses to relieve swelling and pain in joints.

Taken one step further, some people believe that the mineral-rich mud from the Dead Sea is particularly beneficial. However, the few scientific studies made of this therapy are too small to be able to draw any firm conclusions.

Whilst more research is needed to determine if the mineral content of the mud, the mud itself, or just the soothing warmth of the mud compresses helps people's painful joints feel better, this therapy may provide some temporary relief of pain or, at least, relaxation.

Hypnosis

Many people associate hypnosis with carnival entertainment or trickery. But as a serious treatment it dates back a few hundred years, and is utilized by many medical professionals. Hypnosis may be effective for some people in chronic pain. Although some people can hypnotize themselves, it may be easier at first to work with a trained professional, such as a psychiatrist, psychologist or hypnotherapist.

Hypnosis was first employed by Franz Anton Mesmer, an Austrian doctor, who used it to treat patients with various nervous conditions or ailments by lulling them into a state of extreme mental relaxation. This practice, first known as *mesmerism* after its creator, involved the person staring at a light or object until they reached this very relaxed state.

Hypnosis is done much the same way today. In this state, the person is more susceptible to suggestion, and the doctor can help the person learn to relax tense muscles or reduce the stress that may be causing or worsening pain. Hypnosis has been used as a therapy for chronic migraine headaches, as well as other painful conditions.

Ultrasound Therapy

Ultrasound or ultrasonography is used extensively in diagnosis. It also may be used as a therapy: the high-frequency sound waves emit a soothing heat that may be used to relieve muscle or tissue pain. Similar to the heat therapy provided by heating pads or hydrotherapy, ultrasound offers only temporary relief.

A health-care professional (usually a physiotherapist) trained in ultrasound must administer the therapy. Doctors will usually prescribe ultrasound therapy when a person is experiencing a severe flare of pain that may not be adequately relieved by pain medicines. Ultrasound therapy is not recommended for people whose pain is accompanied by inflammation, because the heat might worsen the swelling. But for many people, ultrasound therapy is a useful complement to their pain-management treatments.

A similar type of ultrasound therapy called *shock-wave therapy* was not found to be very

beneficial in a recent Australian study, where people with the painful foot condition plantar fasciitis underwent treatment of shock or sound waves over a three-week period. In the UK, the National Institute for Health and Clinical Excellence is evaluating the value of this therapy in plantar fasciitis. Progress on the evaluation can be found on the NICE web site (see the Resources section for contact details).

Consult your doctor to see if he recommends using this therapy for your pain condition.

Prolotherapy

A relatively new experimental technique for chronic pain relief, *prolotherapy* aims to relieve pain by rebuilding and strengthening weakened connective tissues, particularly ligaments and tendons that may be painful due to injury or continued stress or pressure. Because muscles, ligaments and tendons support the bones, when they weaken you are more susceptible to pain and further injury.

Prolotherapy is often used to treat back pain, neck pain, sciatica or *whiplash*, a common and painful condition where the neck is whipped back and forth suddenly due to an impact, such as a car accident. Prolotherapy is also called sclerotherapy, proliferative injection therapy, stimulated ligament repair, regenerative injection therapy or non-surgical ligament reconstruction. As these names suggest, the therapy is meant to repair or restore the damaged or weakened connective tissues that can no longer properly support joints and bones, leading to pain with every movement. Prolotherapy is usually administered by a doctor.

Prolotherapy differs from other injection therapies, and that's why it's still controversial. In prolotherapy, the doctor injects an irritating solution into the damaged or painful soft tissues. Rather than traditional injections, which use an anti-inflammatory medication, prolotherapy's aim is to *create* inflammation. Why? Proponents of the therapy believe this intentional inflammation will increase blood circulation in the painful area and hasten the healing process. So the small tears or weaknesses in the damaged connective tissues will heal, the tissues will strengthen and the pain will subside. Normally, two or three treatments are given, with a gap of one to four weeks between them.

Prolotherapy is still controversial because there is a lack of research evidence to prove its benefit. However, a small number of randomized clinical trials have shown that it is safe, and may be effective.

Aromatherapy

Sniffing pleasant fragrances is a soothing, relaxing activity, but some people have refined this practice into a treatment called *aromatherapy*. Aromatherapy involves smelling various fragrances from essential oils (concentrated amounts of a fragrance derived from a plant), candles or incense to relax, relieve pain and reduce symptoms. Popular aromatherapy essential oils include eucalyptus, peppermint, rosemary, laurel, chamomile, marjoram, jasmine and lavender. Epsom salts or sea salts may be used in hot aromatherapy baths.

Use of aromatic herbs or incense as a way to heal physical or emotional pain dates back thousands of years. The ancient Egyptians, Chinese, Greeks, Indians and other civilizations used such practices as part of their healing rites. During the Black Death epidemic in medieval Europe, doctors felt that pestilence and disease might spread in foul-smelling air or mists, leading to a practice of wearing masks containing fragrance as a way to purify the air they breathed and protect them from disease.

In 1928, a French practitioner named Rene Maurice Gattefosse coined the term 'aromatherapy' to describe the emerging contemporary practice of using fragrance for healing. Aromatherapy has gained popularity in recent years as a method of relieving stress and healing various problems. However, the term may be misunderstood, applied too broadly or misused. Many product manufacturers use the term aromatherapy to promote any good-smelling product, from candles to room sprays to carpet deodorizers.

Aromatherapy as a pain-relief therapy involves smelling specific scents for certain purposes. You can be aided by an aromatherapy practitioner or therapist, who will administer the treatments or guide you in doing it yourself. Aromatherapy applications include massage with particular oils, steam baths with essential oils added to the steam source, aromatic baths to soak in, inhalation using a cloth or an electronic diffuser, candles, sprays, aromatic rubs or creams and more.

Aromatherapy may not provide effective relief for chronic pain, but some aromatherapy treatments may provide relaxation, easing tense muscles. Hot baths or steam baths might be soothing to sore joints and muscles, and adding the essential oil may provide some additional soothing qualities to the mind. It is important to use any of these treatments properly and with your doctor's knowledge. Some essential oils or creams that come in contact with the skin might cause rashes or other skin irritations. It's important to keep any essential oils or other fragrance sources away from the eyes, particularly sprays that might contain alcohol, chemical propellants or other irritants.

Does aromatherapy really work? Evidence does not yet support the efficacy of this therapy on its own for pain relief, but aromatherapy may provide help in achieving relaxation, leading to easing of tense muscles that can cause pain.

CONTROVERSIAL COMPLEMENTARY THERAPIES

Some other complementary treatments for chronic pain are controversial and spark a division of opinion and debate among doctors and other health-care professionals. Many of these treatments simply may not work, or they may work for some people but not for others. Some people feel that if something can't hurt, it's worth trying. That's up to you. Most therapies involve some cost as well as your time and effort. So saying 'it couldn't hurt' is really not true: if you pay for something that doesn't work and can't easily get a refund for your money, it hurts! You may also feel discouraged by the failed treatment, causing additional stress and anxiety about your chronic pain.

The best way to avoid this situation is to talk to your doctor and ask for advice. You can also conduct some of your own research on the Internet or by reading reputable health journals for reports of study results on various treatments.

Below are a few other treatments for chronic pain that could be considered to be controversial:

Low-level laser therapy. Lasers, beams of highly concentrated light, first appeared in science-fiction movies, but some doctors and physiotherapists treat painful areas of the body with low-level laser beams as a way to stimulate cell growth, boost endorphin production, treat inflammation or promote healing of damaged nerves. It remains uncertain whether this therapy really works for treating chronic pain.

Magnet therapy. The wearing or application of magnets as a method of healing or pain relief is ancient, first used by the Egyptians and Greeks. In recent years, people in pain revived the practice as a way to relieve pain, particularly after injuries, accidents, or in cases of arthritis, fibromyalgia or back pain. Magnets may be worn as a wristband or neck collar or as insoles.

The therapy aims to change the way cells behave or to alter body chemistry to promote healing, but many doctors, scientists and sceptics claim this treatment is bogus – just a ploy to get you to buy a magnet bracelet or device. Research evidence to date cannot demonstrate any benefit from magnet therapy when compared with placebo devices. Many magnets sold in retail stores or through the Internet have no power and probably no benefit, but it is estimated that, world-wide, over £3 billion has been spent on magnet therapy. The future of magnet therapy may lie in more powerful devices that can emit a stronger form of magnetic energy, called pulse electromagnetic therapy. This therapy, rising in popularity, may be more worthwhile.

Gin-soaked raisins. Soaking raisins in gin or other alcoholic beverages and eating them is an old folk remedy for arthritis pain. The gin may offer a temporary dulling of aches, but alcohol is not recommended as a pain reliever. Although they may be tasty, gin-soaked raisins do not offer any real medical benefit.

Marijuana. Marijuana, the common name for the widely grown but illegally (in most countries) sold or used plant *Cannabis sativa,* is highly controversial as an analgesic and anti-nausea treatment. Many battles between the legal, political, medical and patient communities are taking place as some people in chronic pain fight for the option to use marijuana as a medicine. Marijuana, when smoked or ingested, can create an extreme sense of relaxation and pain relief for a time. Yet it can also be psychologically (though not physically)

addictive, and is viewed negatively as a street drug. In the UK it was reclassified as a Class C drug in 2004, although it is still placed within the Misuse of Drugs Regulations as a Schedule 1 drug, implying that it has no medical use.

Some studies show that marijuana may have a positive effect on pain receptors in the brain and help to reduce the brain's pain response, similar to the way analgesic drugs work. In the UK, a cannabinoid drug called nabilone is licensed for medical use but only as an anti-sickness treatment in cancer patients receiving chemotherapy. Although nabilone is a synthetic cannabinoid, it still has many of the effects of cannabis, and may cause psychological addiction. More studies are required to determine if a medical use for marijuana in terms of chronic pain treatment merits its legalization as a substance that can be prescribed by doctors.

YOU DECIDE

Whether you wish to try a complementary treatment for your pain or just stick to more tried-and-true options, there are an increasing number of treatments available to explore. Some of these treatments are less involved or invasive than others, allowing you to try them without significant risk or cost. It's important to be fully informed before you try any complementary treatment, and to tell your doctor whatever you do. In some cases, your doctor can offer you a referral or suggestions about what treatments will work best for your type of pain, and many doctors are open to their patients creating an integrative pain-management plan.

Some treatments that lie outside the realm of drugs or surgery, but are not quite as experimental as those covered in this chapter, are what we call 'do-it-yourself' therapies or lifestyle management techniques. A person in chronic pain needs to create a healthy overall lifestyle to control their daily pain and to manage the underlying disease that causes the pain.

This concept is at the heart of any successful pain-management plan. You will probably hear your doctor tell you that pain medicines won't do the job alone – your actions are also an incredibly powerful weapon in the fight against chronic pain. Exercise, proper diet, relaxation and stress management, learning proper movement and getting proper sleep will help your body to heal injuries, restore energy, increase flexibility and lessen pain. Whilst exercising may be the last thing you want to do when you're in pain, it might be the first thing you should do each day to prevent and reduce pain.

CONCLUSION

As you have learned by reading this book, the prognosis for your life with arthritis is full of hope. Proper treatment, including drugs, surgery, exercise and stress reduction methods, can help relieve the pain and other symptoms you experience. As a result of recent advances in arthritis drug development, you may be able to slow or halt the damage to your joints in some cases. Never before has your doctor had so many options to counter the effects of arthritis. But the most important leader in your arthritis care and management is you. That's the key message of this book. When you take an active role in managing your arthritis, your overall health and well-being will improve dramatically.

Take the medications your doctor prescribes. Tell him or her of any drug-related problems you experience or supplements you take in addition to your prescription medications. Explore the option of surgery if it is appropriate. Take action steps that will reduce your pain: exercise, heat and cold treatments, massage therapy, acupuncture, water-exercise (aquarobics) classes, weight loss, stress reduction. Refer to the guidelines in this book to help you manage your arthritis, instead of letting your disease manage your life.

Whether you are newly diagnosed with arthritis or have lived with arthritis for years, information is available to help you travel every step of your journey. In addition to this book, Arthritis Care is a great place to begin finding the guidance and support you need. The following section is a brief summary of the publications, programmes and services this organization offers to help people with arthritis take control. With the tools you have from reading this book and the resources of your regional Arthritis Care office, you can manage your arthritis and live a full, abundant life.

Resources

Resources | The Arthritis Foundation

The Arthritis Foundation is the only US-wide, nonprofit health organization helping people take greater control of arthritis by leading efforts to prevent, control and cure arthritis and related diseases – the nation's number one cause of disability. Nearly 66 million Americans currently have arthritis or a related condition – and that number is expected to grow in the coming years. To serve this population, Arthritis Foundation volunteers and staff nationwide provide information, programmes, services and research assistance.

The Arthritis Foundation's efforts centre on the three-fold mission of the organization: research, prevention and quality of life. Since its founding in 1948, the Arthritis Foundation has distributed more than $350 million to help support research for new treatments for arthritis and related diseases. The Arthritis Foundation's sponsorship of research for more than 50 years has resulted in major treatment advances for most arthritis-related diseases.

You have learned more about these diseases and their many treatments in this book.

The Arthritis Foundation, which has more than 100 chapters and branch offices to serve people with arthritis in communities nationwide, provides a number of community-based programmes and services. In addition, Arthritis Foundation volunteers serve as advocates to local and national governments on behalf of people with arthritis. Their successes include the federal establishment of a national institute for arthritis among the National Institutes of Health, increased federal funding for arthritis research and state funding for arthritis medications. The Arthritis Foundation has an array of award-winning publications, including the bimonthly magazine *Arthritis Today*; a number of books, brochures and subscription newsletters; and an interactive web site, **www.arthritis.org**, which offers a wealth of information about arthritis, current research and advocacy-related news, and an interactive self-management programme, *Connect and Control*.

Resources | Arthritis Care

Arthritis Care is the largest UK-wide voluntary organisation working with and for all people with arthritis. We aim to promote independence and empower people with arthritis to live positive lives as well as raise awareness of the condition. We have over 300 branches and groups, and over 70,000 supporters.

Arthritis Care:

- provides a help service by email, telephone and letter, weekdays 12 noon–4pm on a freephone helpline (0808 800 4050). It is also available 10am–4pm charged at the national rate. Tel: 020 7380 6555. Email: Helplines@arthritiscare.org.uk

- offers The Source, a helpline service for young people with arthritis and their families by telephone, letter and email.

  Freephone: 0808 808 2000
  weekdays 10am–2pm

  Email: thesource@arthritiscare.org.uk

- produces a range of helpful publications including:
  a bi-monthly magazine, *Arthritis News*

Information for People with Arthritis
Living with Arthritis
Living with Rheumatoid Arthritis
The Balanced Approach
Talk About Pain
Surgery
Fit for Life
Food for Thought
Working Horizons
Our Feelings, Our Emotions
Our Relationships, Our Sexuality

To order, call 020 7380 6540; or download from our web site:
www.arthritiscare.org.uk

- offers a range of self-management and personal development training courses for people with arthritis of all ages to enable people to be in control of their arthritis

- runs four hotels in the UK

- campaigns for greater awareness of the needs of all people with arthritis

- has a network of staff and volunteers across the UK, and has offices in England, Wales, Scotland and Northern Ireland. Phone 020 7380 6540 to find your nearest one.

Action on Pain
20 Necton Road
Little Dunham PE32 2DN
Helpline: 0845 603 1593
(Mon–Fri, 9am–5pm)
Tel: 01760 725993
Web site: www.action-on-pain.co.uk
*Provides support for people with
chronic pain, and their families
or carers.*

Arthritis Care
18 Stephenson Way
London NW1 2HD
Helplines: 0800 800 4050
(Mon–Fri, noon–4pm)
020 7380 6555
(Mon–Fri, 10am–4pm)
Helpline for young people and
their families: 0808 808 2000
(Mon–Fri, 10am–2pm)
Fax: 020 7380 6505
Web site: www.arthritiscare.org.uk
*Provides information and support
to enable people to live with and
manage arthritis. Campaigns for
greater awareness and better
services. The helpline is the first
port of call for anyone with
arthritis.Many small organisations
for particular types of arthritis; for
details ring the helpline or
Freephone 0808 800 4050*

**Arthritis Foundation
of Ireland**
1 Clanwilliam Square
Grand Canal Quay
Dublin 2
Ireland
Tel: 00 353 1 66 18188
Fax: 00 353 1 66 18261
Web site: www.arthritis-foundation.com
*General information and support
with educational lectures. Local
support groups run information
and fundraising events.*

Arthritis Research Campaign
Copeman House
St Mary's Court
St Mary's Gate
Chesterfield S41 7TD
Tel: 01246 558 033
Fax: 01246 558 007
Web site: www.arc.org.uk
*Finances an extensive programme
of research and education in a
wide range of arthritis and
rheumatism problems, including
back pain. Has useful booklets
explaining related problems and
ways of coping with them.*

BackCare
16 Elmtree Road
Teddington TW11 8ST
Tel: 020 8977 5474
Fax: 020 8943 5318
Web site: www.backcare.org.uk
*Information and advice for people
with back pain. Funds patient-
orientated scientific research into
the causes, treatment and
prevention of back pain. Has local
support groups throughout the
country with regular meetings.*

Benefits Enquiry Line
Tel: 0800 88 22 00
Northern Ireland: 0800 220 674
Textphone: 0800 243 355
Web site: www.dwp.gov.uk
*Government agency giving
information about state benefits
for sick or disabled people and
their carers.*

British Acupuncture Council
63 Jeddo Road
London W12 9HQ
Tel: 020 8735 0400
Fax: 020 8735 0404
Web site: www.acupuncture.org.uk
*Professional body offering lists of
qualified acupuncture therapists.*

British Homeopathic Association
Hahnemann House
29 Park Street West
Luton LU1 3BE
Tel: 08704 443 950
Fax: 08704 443 960
Web site: www.trusthomeopathy.org
*Professional body offering lists of
qualified homoeopathic
practitioners.*

**British Society
for Rheumatology**
41 Eagle Street
London WC1R 4TL
Tel: 020 7242 3313
Fax: 020 7242 3277
Web site: www.rheumatology.org.uk
*Professional membership body
representing rheumatologists.*

**British Sjögren's Syndrome
Association**
PO Box 10867
Birmingham B16 0ZW
Helpline: 0121 455 6549
(Mon–Thu, 9.30am–4.30pm)
Tel (admin): 0121 455 6532
(Mon–Fri, 9am–5pm)
Web site: www.bssa.uk.net
*Self-help group giving
information and advice on how to
alleviate the symptoms of Sjögren's
syndrome; publishes a quarterly
newsletter.*

Carers UK
20–25 Glasshouse Yard
London EC1A 4JS
Helpline: 0808 808 7777
(Mon–Fri, 10am–noon; 2–4pm)
Tel: 020 7490 8818
Fax: 020 7490 8824
Web site: www.carersonline.org.uk
*Provides a wide range of
information and support to all
carers.*

**Chartered Society
of Physiotherapy**
14 Bedford Road
London WC1R 4ED
Tel: 020 7306 6666
Fax: 020 7306 6611
Web site: www.csp.org.uk
*For information about all aspects
of physiotherapy; offers list of
chartered physiotherapists in your
area.*

**Children's Chronic Arthritis
Association**
Ground Floor
Amber Gate
City Wall Road
Worcester WR1 2AH
Tel: 01905 745 595
Fax: 01905 745 703
Web site: www.ccaa.org.uk
*Offers practical information
to maximise choices and
opportunities and raise awareness
of childhood arthritis in the
community. A support network
run by parents offers emotional
support; runs a yearly family
week-end conference.*

**CHOICES for Families
of Children with Arthritis**
PO Box 58
Hove
East Sussex BN3 5WN
Web site: www.kidswitharthritis.org
*Provides information for children
with arthritis and their families
about living with arthritis. Also
provides an education resource to
enhance health and social care,
community and education
services.*

Department of Health
PO Box 777
London SE1 6HX
Helpline: 0800 555 777
Tel: 020 7210 4850
Textphone: 020 7210 3000
Fax: 01623 724 524
Web site: www.doh.gov.uk
*Produces literature about all
health issues, including
prescription charges and
prepayment certificates, available
via the Helpline. A more
technical site, with National
Service Frameworks, is available
at www.doh.gov.uk/nsf/arthritis.*

**Department for Work
and Pensions**
Benefits Enquiry Line:
0800 88 22 00
Tel: 020 7712 2171
Textphone: 0800 24 33 55
Fax: 020 7712 2386
Web site: www.dwp.gov.uk
*Government department giving
information about, and claim
forms for, all state benefits.*

Disability Alliance
Universal House
88–94 Wentworth Street
London E1 7SA
Helpline: 020 7247 8765
(Mon & Wed, 2–4pm)
Tel: 020 7247 8776 (voice
and textphone)
Fax: 020 7247 8763
Web site: www.disabilityalliance.org
*Information on welfare benefits
entitlement, to people with
disabilities, their families, carers
and professional advisers. Services
include advice, campaign work,
research and training.*

Disability Sport England
N17 Studio, Unit 4G
784–788 High Road
London N17 0DA
Tel: 020 8801 4466
Fax: 020 8801 6644
Web site: www.disabilitysport.org.uk
*National events agency that
encourages sport for people of all
ages with disabilities from local to
national level.*

**Disabled Living Centres
Council**
Redbank House
4 St Chad's Street
Manchester M8 8QA
Tel: 0161 834 1044
Textphone: 0161 839 0885
Fax: 0161 839 0802
Web site: www.dlcc.org.uk
*For a Centre near you, where you
can see furniture, aids and equip-
ment for elderly and disabled
people. Offers training courses for
health professionals; information
leaflets available on request.*

Disabled Living Foundation
380–384 Harrow Road
London W9 2HU
Helpline: 0845 130 1977
Tel: 020 7289 6111
Textphone: 020 7432 8009
Fax: 020 7266 2922
Web site: www.dlf.org.uk
*Provides information to disabled
and elderly people on all kinds of
equipment in order to promote
their independence and quality
of life.*

**European League against
Rheumatism (EULAR)**
Eular Executive Secretariat
Witikonerstrasse 15
CH 8032 Zurich, Switzerland
Tel: + 41 1 383 9690
Fax: + 41 1 383 9810
Web site: www.eular.org
*Publishes journals, holds
international conferences; web site
shows images of different diseases.
Provides up-to-date information
for professionals and patient
organizations.*

Fibromyalgia Association UK
PO Box 206
Stourbridge DY9 8YL
Tel: 0870 220 1232
Fax: 0870 752 5118
Web site:
www.fibromyalgia-associationuk.org
*Provides information for patients
with fibromyalgia and has a
network of local support groups
throughout the UK. Campaigns
for a better recognition and
awareness of the disorder.*

General Osteopathic Council
Osteopathy House
176 Tower Bridge Road
London SE1 3LU
Tel: 020 7357 6655
Fax: 020 7357 0011
Web site: www.osteopathy.org.uk
*Regulatory body that offers
information to the public and lists
of accredited osteopaths.*

Independent Living Fund
PO Box 7525
Nottingham NG2 4ZT
Helpline: 0845 601 8815
Tel: 0115 942 8191
Fax: 0115 945 0948
Web site: www.ilf.org.uk
*May provide top-up funding for
very severely disabled people to
buy in extra personal and/or
domestic care. Applicants must
already be receiving the higher
care allowance and at least £200
care package from Social Services.
Referral via Social Services.*

Joint Zone
Web site: www.jointzone.org.uk
*Free educational web site, funded
by the Arthritis Research
Campaign, International League
of Associations for Rheumatology
and others, intended mainly for
medical students, with
information about various forms
of arthritis and treatments. Gives
case studies and lectures.*

Lupus UK
St James House
Eastern Road
Romford
Essex RM1 3NH
Tel: 01708 731251
Fax: 01708 731252
Web site: www.lupusuk.com
*Offers support, advice and
information for people with
systemic lupus erythematosus.*

**MAVIS (Mobility Advice
and Vehicle Information
Service)**
Department for Transport
Crowthorne Business Estate
Old Wokingham Road
Crowthorne
Berkshire RG45 6XD
Tel: 01344 661000
Fax: 01344 661066
Web site: www.mobility-unit.dft.gov.uk
*Government department offering
driving and vehicle assessments
and advice for people with
mobility problems. Can advise
on vehicle adaptations for both
drivers and passengers.*

Motability
Goodman House
Station Approach
Harlow
Essex CM20 2ET
Helpline: 01279 635 666
(Mon–Fri, 8.45am–5.15pm)
Tel: 01279 635 999 (admin)
Textphone: 01279 632 273
Fax: 01279 632 000
Web site: www.motability.co.uk
*Advises people with disabilities
about powered wheelchairs,
scooters, and new and used cars,
how to adapt them to their needs
and how to obtain funding via
the Mobility Scheme.*

**National Ankylosing
Spondylitis Society (NASS)**
PO Box 179
Mayfield
East Sussex TN20 6ZL
Tel: 01435 873 527
Fax: 01435 873 027
Web site: www.nass.co.uk
*Provides information and advice
to patients with ankylosing
spondylitis, their families and
professionals. Has over 100
branches providing supervised
physiotherapy one evening a week.
Video and cassette tapes of
physiotherapy exercises available.*

**National Centre for
Independent Living**
250 Kennington Lane
London SE11 5RD
Tel: 020 7587 1663
Textphone: 020 7587 1177
Fax: 020 7582 2469
Web site: www.ncil.org.uk
*Provides advice on independent
living and Direct Payments, and
details of your local Centre for
Independent Living, to enable
people to buy private personal
and/or domestic care instead of
receiving it via the local authority.*

NHS Direct
Tel: 0845 46 47
Textphone: 0845 606 4647
NHS24 (Scotland):
0800 22 44 88
Web site: www.nhsdirect.nhs.uk
*First point of contact to find out
about NHS services and for any
health advice, which is available
24 hours daily, 365 days a year.*

National Osteoporosis Society
Camerton
Bath
Somerset BA2 0PJ
Helpline: 0845 450 0230
Tel: 01761 471 771
Fax: 01761 471 104
Web site: www.nos.org.uk
*Provides information and advice
on all aspects of osteoporosis,
the menopause and hormone
replacement therapy. Encourages
people to take action to protect
their bones. Helpline staffed by
specially trained nurses. Has
local support groups.*

Pain Society
21 Portland Place
London W1B 1PY
Tel: 020 7631 8870
Fax: 020 7323 2015
Web site: www.painsociety.org
*Primarily for health care
professionals; publishes*
Understanding and Managing
Pain *for patients.*

Patients Association
PO Box 935
Harrow
Middlesex HA1 3YJ
Helpline: 0845 608 4455
(Mon–Fri, 10am–4pm)
Tel (admin): 020 8423 9111
(Mon–Fri, 9am–5pm)
Fax: 020 8423 9119
Web site: www.patients-association.com
*Gives advice on patients' rights,
complaints procedures and access
to health services or appropriate
self-help groups.*

**Prince of Wales's Foundation
for Integrated Health**
12 Chillingworth Road
London N7 8QJ
Tel: 020 7619
Fax: 020 7700 8434
Web site: www.fihealth.org.uk
*Encourages conventional and
complementary practitioners to
work together to integrate their
approaches to health care; provides
information, education and
research and development.*

Psoriatic Arthropathy Alliance
PO Box 111
St Albans AL2 3JQ
Tel: 0870 770 3212
Fax: 0870 770 3213
Web site: www.paalliance.org
*Raises awareness of psoriatic
arthropathy. Provides information, produces a regular journal
and puts people in touch with one
another. You don't have to be a
member if you wish to receive
information.*

**RADAR (Royal Association
for Disability and
Rehabilitation)**
12 City Forum
250 City Road
London EC1V 8AF
Tel: 020 7250 3222
Textphone: 020 7250 4119
Fax: 020 7250 0212
Web site: www.radar.org.uk
*Information about aids and
mobility, holidays, sport and
leisure for disabled people.
Campaigns to improve the rights
and care of disabled people. Sells
special key to access locked
disabled toilets.*

REMAP
National Organiser
'Hazeldene'
Ightham
Sevenoaks
Kent TN15 9AD
Tel: 0845 1300 456
Fax: 0845 1300 789
Web site: www.remap.org.uk
*Makes or adapts aids, when not
commercially available, for people
with disabilities, at no charge to
the disabled person.
Has local branches.*

St Thomas' Lupus Trust
The Rayne Institute
St Thomas' Hospital
London SE1 7EH
Tel: 020 7188 3562
Fax: 020 7188 3574
Web site: www.lupus.org.uk
*Supports both research into lupus
and the Louise Coote Lupus Unit
and provides information both to
professionals and to people who
have the condition.*

Glossary

Glossary

A

ACUPUNCTURE – Eastern medicine technique in which thin needles are used to puncture the body at specific sites along energy pathways (meridians). Although still widely considered an alternative therapy, acupuncture is gaining acceptance in Western medicine, primarily for use in pain relief. Acupressure is another form of this treatment, but one involving hand pressure rather than needle punctures.

ACUTE ILLNESS – An illness of short duration that comes on quickly and produces severe symptoms.

ANAESTHESIA – The induction of partial or complete loss of sensation. Used to perform surgery and other medical procedures.

ANALGESIC – A type of medication used to treat pain.

ANKYLOSING SPONDYLITIS (AS) – A form of arthritis that mainly affects the spine and sacroiliac joints (where the spine attaches to the pelvis). In severe cases, AS may cause the spine to become fused and rigid.

ANTINUCLEAR ANTIBODIES (ANA) – Proteins produced by the immune system against the cell nucleus (control centre). They are often present in people with certain forms of the arthritis, including lupus and scleroderma. A test showing a positive ANA can help a doctor in diagnosis.

ARTHRODESIS – A surgical procedure in which the two bones that form a joint are fused into a single, immovable unit.

ARTHROPLASTY – Also called joint replacement surgery, a procedure in which a damaged joint is surgically removed and replaced with an artificial one.

ARTHROSCOPY – A surgical procedure in which a thin, lighted scope is inserted into the joint through a small incision or puncture site, allowing the joint's interior to be viewed on a monitor. Through additional small incisions, tools can be inserted to do minor surgical repairs such as smoothing rough cartilage or removing cartilage fragments.

ASPIRATION – The withdrawal of fluid from the body, such as synovial fluid from the joint.

AUTOIMMUNE DISEASE – A disease in which the immune system, which is designed to protect the body from foreign invaders such as viruses and bacteria, instead turns against the body and causes damage to the body's healthy tissue.

B

BIOFEEDBACK – The use of electronic instruments to measure body functions and feed that information back to you, allowing you to learn how to control body processes, such as heart rate or blood pressure, that are generally thought to be out of conscious control.

BIOLOGICAL FIXATION – A process by which joint prostheses with specially designed, porous surfaces are held in place by the growth of patients' own bone into the prostheses.

BIOLOGICAL RESPONSE MODIFIERS – Drugs that target and modify specific pathways involved in the development of disease. The current biological response modifiers used for rheumatoid arthritis target specific immune system chemicals, called cytokines, that play a role in the inflammation and damage of the disease, while leaving other immune-system components intact.

BIOPSY – A procedure to remove a piece of tissue for study. Depending on the piece of tissue examined, your doctor may use a biopsy to diagnose diseases of the joint, muscle, skin or blood vessels.

BISPHOSPHONATES – A class of medications that inhibit bone resorption (see below) and are used to treat bone diseases such as osteoporosis.

BONE FUSION – The growth of two bones into a solid, immobile unit. Surgeons often promote bone fusion by removing the cartilage from two bones at a joint and then holding them in place by a cast, splint or pins until the bones grow together. Joint fusion offers pain relief for joints that typically aren't replaced with prostheses.

BONE RESORPTION – The loss of bone through physiological means. In the body, existing bone is constantly being resorbed while new bone grows to take its place. Bone resorption is essential to healthy bones unless it outpaces the growth of new bone.

BOUCHARD'S NODES – Knobby growths of bone that commonly appear on the middle knuckle in people with osteoarthritis.

BURSAE – Small, fluid-filled sacs that cushion and lubricate joints.

BURSITIS – Inflammation of the bursae (fluid-filled sacs that lubricate the joints), which can cause pain, tenderness and stiffness of the nearby joint.

C

CAPSAICIN – A pain-relieving substance derived from cayenne pepper that is the active ingredient in some analgesic rubs.

CARPAL TUNNEL SYNDROME – Compression of the median nerve, which supplies the thumbside of the hand as it enters the palm. Often caused by inflammation in the carpal tunnel, the space between bones of the wrist through which the nerve and tendons run, it can cause numbness of the middle and index finger and weakness of the thumb.

CARTILAGE – A smooth, rubbery tissue that covers the ends of the bones at the joints and acts as a shock absorber, allowing the joint to move smoothly.

CHIROPODY – see Podiatry

CHIROPRACTIC – Practice of healing based on spinal manipulation and the belief that illness stems from malalignment of the vertebrae.

CHRONIC ILLNESS – An illness of long duration, possibly a lifetime.

COLLAGEN – A protein that is the primary component of cartilage and other connective tissue.

COMPLEMENT – A protein in the blood involved in certain forms of inflammation. Complement levels are often low in people with systemic lupus erythematosus, for example.

CORTICOSTEROIDS – A group of hormones, including cortisol, produced by the adrenal glands. They can be synthetically produced (that is, made in a laboratory) and have powerful anti-inflammatory effects. They are sometimes called just steroids.

COX-2 SPECIFIC INHIBITOR – A type of non-steroidal anti-inflammatory drug (NSAID) that is designed to be safer for the stomach than other NSAIDs. COX-2 inhibitors work by inhibiting hormone-like substances in the body that cause pain and inflammation without interfering with similar substances that protect the stomach lining.

CYTOKINES – Chemical messengers in the body that play a role in the immune response.

D

DERMATOMYOSITIS – The disease in which generally muscle weakness is accompanied by a skin rash (see Polymyositis).

DEXA – Short for dual-energy X-ray absorptiometry, a scan that measures bone density at the hip and spine to diagnose osteoporosis and evaluate bone density.

DMARDS – Short for disease-modifying antirheumatic drugs, a class of medications that work to modify the course of rheumatoid arthritis and other forms of inflammatory arthritis, slowing or even stopping its progression.

Glossary

E

EPIDURAL ANAESTHESIA – Anaesthetic injected directly into the spinal canal, between the spinal column and the outermost cover of the spinal cord. Epidural anaesthesia is used to numb the lower half of the body and is often used in knee surgery.

EROSIONS – A wearing away of the bone in the joint caused by inflammation of the joint lining.

ERYTHROCYTE SEDIMENTATION RATE (ESR) – Also referred to as sed rate, a test measuring how fast red blood cells (erythrocytes) clump together and fall to the bottom of a test tube like sediment. A high (fast) sedimentation rate signals the presence of inflammation, possibly indicating an inflammatory disease such as rheumatoid arthritis.

F

FATIGUE – A generalized, long-lasting feeling of tiredness or sleepiness that isn't relieved by sleep or rest.

FIBROMYALGIA – A syndrome characterized by widespread muscle pain, the presence of tender points (or points on the body that feel painful on pressure) and often debilitating fatigue and other symptoms.

G

GOUT – A form of arthritis that occurs when uric acid builds up in the blood and is deposited as crystals in the joints and other tissue. A joint, such as the big toe, affected by gout may be excruciatingly painful, and shiny and purplish in appearance.

H

HAMMER TOES – Toes that are dislocated and look like the hammers in a piano. The problem is often seen in people with RA and results in ulcers on the tops of the toes and pain when walking.

HEBERDEN'S NODES – Knobby growths of bone that may appear on the knuckles nearest the nails in people with osteoarthritis.

HYALURONIC ACID – A substance in the synovial fluid of the joints that gives the fluid its viscosity and shock-absorbing properties.

I

IMMUNE SYSTEM – The body's natural system of defence against invaders, such as viruses and bacteria, that it sees as harmful.

INFLAMMATION – An immune-system response to injury or infection that causes heat, redness and swelling in the affected area. In some forms of arthritis, joint and organ inflammation occurs as a result of a faulty immune response to the body's own tissues.

J

JOINT – The juncture of two or more bones in the body. The human body contains more than 150 joints, some of which are rigid and others that allow the body to move in many different positions.

JUVENILE IDIOPATHIC ARTHRITIS – A type of arthritis that occurs in children under age 16. There are three different forms of JIA, differentiated primarily by the number of joints they affect.

L

LIGAMENTS – Tough bands of connective tissue that attach bones to bones and help keep them together at a joint.

LUPUS – A term often used to refer to systemic lupus erythematosus, an autoimmune disease that can affect the joints, skin, blood, lungs, kidneys, and cardiovascular and nervous systems.

M

MRI – Short for magnetic resonance imaging, MRI is a procedure in which a very strong magnet is used to pass a force through the body to create a clear, detailed image of a cross-section of the body.

MUSCLE – Fibrous tissue in the body holds us upright and gives the body movement, including both movement that we consciously initiate (such as waving a hand) and movement of which we are scarcely aware (such movement of the blood through the vessels or food through the digestive system).

N

NON-STEROIDAL ANTI-INFLAMMATORY DRUGS (NSAIDS) – A class of medications commonly used to ease the pain and inflammation of many forms of arthritis.

O

OCCUPATIONAL THERAPIST (OT) – A licensed health-care professional who is trained to evaluate the impact of arthritis on daily activities. OTs can help devise easier ways to perform activities that put less stress on fragile joints and can prescribe splints and assistive devices.

OPIATE – A drug used to relieve severe pain by depressing brain function. The name is used particularly for morphine and other derivatives of opium.

ORTHOPAEDIC SURGEON – A doctor who specializes in surgery involving the musculoskeletal system, including the bones and joints

ORTHOTIST – A paramedical health professional who designs, fabricates and fits orthotic devices, such as splints, braces and shoe inserts, to help people function better.

OSTEOARTHRITIS (OA) – The most common form of arthritis. OA causes cartilage breakdown at certain joints (including the spine, hands, hips and knees) resulting in pain and deformity.

OSTEOPOROSIS – A condition in which the body loses so much bone mass that bones are susceptible to disabling fractures under the slightest trauma.

OSTEOTOMY – A surgical procedure that involves cutting and repositioning a bone, usually performed in cases of severe joint malalignment.

P

PAEDIATRIC RHEUMATOLOGIST – A doctor who specializes in treating arthritis and related conditions in children.

PHYSIOTHERAPIST (PHYSIO) – A licensed health-care professional who specializes in using exercise and massage to treat medical conditions. A physio may prescribe canes and splints.

PLACEBO EFFECT – The phenomenon in which a person receiving an inactive drug or therapy experiences a reduction in symptoms.

PODAGRA – Inflammation of the foot, particularly the big toe, caused by gout, a form of arthritis that occurs when uric acid builds up in the blood and is deposited as crystals in the joints and other tissue.

PODIATRY – The treatment of conditions of the foot, from nail infections to arthritis-damaged joints.

POLYMYALGIA RHEUMATICA – A disease causing joint and muscle pain in the neck, shoulders and hips and a general feeling of malaise. The disease is usually marked by a high ESR (see erythrocyte sedimentation rate) and occasionally by a fever.

POLYMYOSITIS – An arthritis-related disease in which generalized weakness results from inflammation of the muscles, primarily those of the shoulders, upper arms, thighs and hips. When muscle weakness is accompanied by a skin rash, the diagnosis is dermatomyositis.

Glossary

PRACTICE NURSE AND NURSE PRACTITIONER – Practice nurses and nurse practitioners are registered nurses with advanced training and emphasis in primary care, who can diagnose illness and, in some cases, prescribe medication.

PROSTAGLANDINS – Hormone-like substances in the body that play a role in pain and inflammation among other body functions.

PROTEIN A IMMUNOADSORPTION THERAPY – A treatment for rheumatoid arthritis that involves filtering the blood plasma through a special column to remove antibodies associated with RA.

PSORIATIC ARTHRITIS – A form of arthritis that is accompanied by the skin disease psoriasis.

Q

QI GONG – An Asian practice that incorporates meditation, breathing exercises and movement to promote health and self-healing.

R

RANGE OF MOVEMENT – The distance and angles at which your joints can be moved, extended and rotated in various directions.

RAYNAUD'S PHENOMENON – A condition in which the blood vessels in the hands go into spasms in response to stress or cold temperatures, resulting in pain, tingling and numbness.

REACTIVE ARTHRITIS – A form of arthritis that occurs when a blood-borne infection settles in a joint or joints.

RESECTION – A surgical procedure that involves removing all or part of a bone, sometimes used to relieve joint pain and stiffness.

REVISION – A second or subsequent operation done to correct problems with a joint prosthesis that has broken, loosened or become infected.

RHEUMATIC DISEASE – A general term referring to conditions characterized by pain and stiffness of the joints or muscles. There are more than 200 rheumatic diseases. The term is often used interchangeably with 'arthritis' (meaning joint inflammation), but not all rheumatic diseases affect the joints or involve inflammation.

RHEUMATISM – A term used loosely (though not as widely used as it was in the past) to refer to conditions that cause pain and swelling in the joints and supporting tissues.

RHEUMATOID ARTHRITIS – A chronic inflammatory form of arthritis in which the body's otherwise protective immune system turns against the body and attacks tissues of the joints, causing pain, inflammation and deformity.

RHEUMATOID FACTOR (RF) – A blood protein (antibody) that is found in high levels in many people with rheumatoid arthritis. It is often associated with RA severity or disease activity, and its presence can be helpful to a doctor in making a diagnosis.

RHEUMATOLOGIST – A doctor who specializes in treating arthritis and related diseases.

RISK/BENEFIT RATIO – The comparison of a treatment's risk of causing adverse effects (and the severity of those effects) to the treatment's potential benefit to the patient. Risks and benefits must be weighed for all treatments a person is considering.

S

SACROILIAC – The joints where the spine attaches to the pelvis.

SALICYLATES – A subcategory of non-steroidal anti-inflammatory drugs (NSAIDs), which includes aspirin. Also describes topical creams containing salicylic acid that relieve pain and inflammation.

SCLERODERMA – An umbrella term for several diseases that involve the abnormal growth of connective tissue. In most cases, the effects of this overgrowth are limited to the skin and underlying tissues, but in others, tissue overgrowth can affect the joints, blood vessels and internal organs.

SED RATE – see Erythrocyte sedimentation rate.

SERMS (SELECTIVE [O]ESTROGEN RECEPTOR MOLECULES) – A class of medications that work much like oestrogen to slow bone loss, but lack oestrogen's side effects on uterine and breast tissues.

SEROSITIS – Inflammation of the lining of some of the organs such as the heart and lungs.

SJÖGREN'S SYNDROME – An arthritis-related disease in which the immune system attacks moisture-producing glands of the body, causing dryness of the eyes, mouth and vagina.

SPLINT – Devices made from metal, plastic, cloth or mouldable foam that are used to support or stabilize a joint or to position a joint in a way that prevents further irritation or injury to joint or soft tissues surrounding it

SPONDYLARTHROPATHIES – A group of arthritis-related diseases that primarily affect the spine.

STEM CELLS – Progenitor cells in the body that have the ability to differentiate into different cells. Some experimental therapies for some autoimmune diseases involve removing stem cells from the body and freezing them; destroying damaging cells; and then reinfusing healthy stem cells back into the body to regrow and replace the damaging cells that were destroyed.

SYNOVECTOMY – Surgical removal of a diseased joint lining (see synovium).

SYNOVIAL FLUID – A slippery liquid secreted by the synovium that lubricates the joint, making movement easier.

SYNOVIUM – A thin membrane that lines the joint capsule and can become inflamed in rheumatoid arthritis.

SYSTEMIC – A term used to refer to anything, such as a disease or medication, that affects the whole body. Rheumatoid arthritis, for example, is a systemic disease.

T

TAI CHI – An ancient Chinese practice that involves gentle, fluid movements and meditation to help strengthen muscles, improve balance and relieve stress

TENDER POINTS – Specific, precise areas on the body that are particularly painful upon the application of slight pressure. The finding of tender points is useful in the diagnosis of fibromyalgia.

TENDINITIS – Painful inflammation of a tendon often caused by injury or over-use, and less frequently by infection or a form of arthritis such as rheumatoid arthritis or ankylosing spondylitis.

TENDONS – Thick connective tissue that attaches the muscles to the bones.

TENS – The acronym for transcutaneous electrical nerve stimulation, this is a treatment for pain that uses a small device to direct mild electric pulses to nerves in the painful area.

TUMOUR NECROSIS FACTOR (TNF) – A cytokine (chemical messenger) in the body that plays a role in inflammation and tissue destruction in diseases such as rheumatoid arthritis, but is also important for normal function of the immune system. Blocking TNF with biologically derived drugs has proven to ease symptoms and inhibit joint destruction in RA.

U

URIC ACID – A bodily waste product that is excreted through the kidneys. When the body produces too much uric acid or doesn't excrete it efficiently, excess uric acid can deposit as crystals in the joint and other tissues, a condition known as gout (see Gout).

URINALYSIS – The analysis of urine using physical, chemical and microscopic tests to detect the presence of infection, levels or uric acid excreted or abnormal constituents.

V

VASCULITIS – Inflammation of the blood vessels that can be a complication of some forms of inflammatory forms of arthritis and related conditions.

VISCOSUPPLEMENTS – Products injected into osteoarthritis joints to replace hyaluronic acid that usually gives the joint fluid its viscosity. This process is known as visco-supplementation.

Y

YOGA – An ancient Indian practice that involves a series of body postures and includes exercise, meditation and breathing components to improve posture and balance and help relieve stress on the joints, as well as emotional stress.